A PHOTOGRAPHIC HISTORY OF PORTSMOUTH

FAREHAM · GOSPORT · HAVANT · HORNDEAN · WATERLOOVILLE

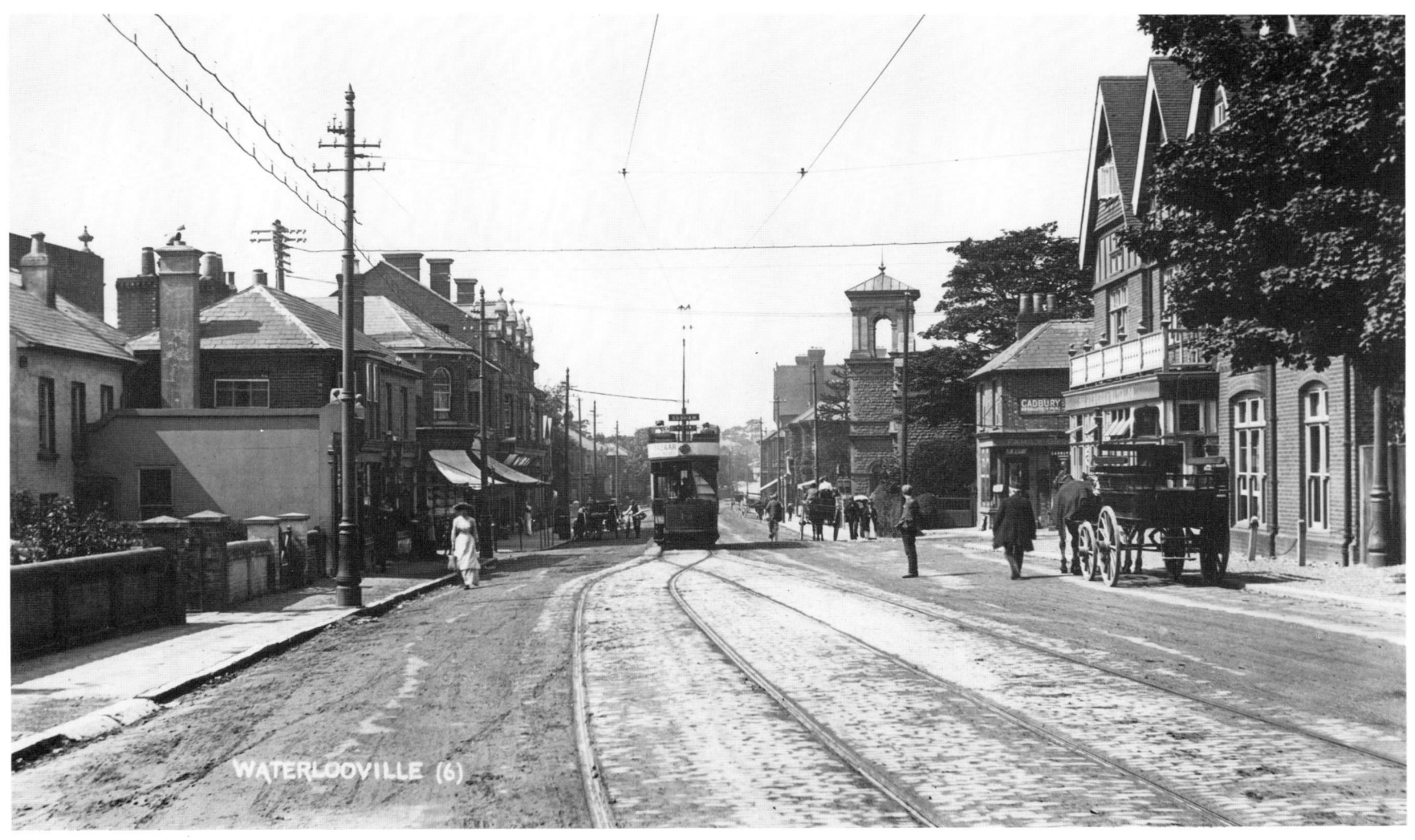

WATERLOOVILLE (6)

ESPLANADE SOUTHSEA

A PHOTOGRAPHIC HISTORY OF PORTSMOUTH

FAREHAM · GOSPORT · HAVANT · HORNDEAN · WATERLOOVILLE

ANTHONY TRIGGS

L. R. P. S.

Ensign

© **Copyright Anthony Triggs 1992.**

First published in 1992 by
Ensign Publications
a division of Hampshire Books Ltd.,
2 Redcar Street,
Southampton SO1 5LL.

Designed and typeset by Precinct Press.
Cover design by The Design Laboratory.
Publisher David Graves.
Photographs reproduced by Plan B, Chandlers Ford.
Text film reproduction by Saxon, Derby.
Printed by Printer Portuguesa, Lisbon.

ISBN 185455 049 7

Half-title page : WATERLOOVILLE CROSSROADS, 1908. A superb Herbert Marshall view with the obligatory tram. The picture shows the short length of double tram track outside the Heroes of Waterloo. Passengers would go into the middle of the road to board the tram. In the background is the impressive Italianate-style spire of the baptist church, built in 1884, mostly through the generosity of the Lancaster family, who had settled in Waterlooville. In 1919 a memorial clock was placed in the tower to commemorate those who died in the 1914-18 war.

Title page : CLARENCE PARADE, SOUTHSEA, 1890. When in 1827 the Duke of Clarence (William IV) visited Portsmouth as Lord High Admiral, he remarked in the hearing of his son, Lord Frederick Fitzclarence, that Southsea beach would make an admirable promenade. Twenty years later when Frederick became Governor of Portsmouth he fulfilled his father's dream, with the help of a Treasury grant, a public subscription and a large quantity of mud from the old steam basin. Clarence Parade is named in his honour and the memorial to the event can still be seen.

Contents page : WEST STREET, HAVANT, 1910. This evocative picture shows a Havant very different to that of today. The dairyman's horse-drawn cart stands outside the post office, where the owner is delivering milk from a huge churn. The wall sign for the Bear Hotel, which of course is still standing, can be seen in the distance. Two doors away from the hotel is Collins' grocers and Italian warehouse, and next door to that a tea room. The dresses of the women shoppers indicate that the picture was taken on a warm day, as does the shadow cast by the premises of C. Pullen the corn merchant on the extreme right.

A c k n o w l e d g e m e n t s

WHEN COMPILING a book of this nature, the most important aspect is researching the photographs, for I have attempted to use those of the best possible quality, rather than the more usual copies of commercial postcards. The great majority have come from my own collection, put together over a period of many years, while others have been supplied by organizations and individuals and I would like to pay tribute to them for their help and kindness

The Royal Commission on the Historical Monuments of England; the Imperial War Museum; Kay Edney; Steve Bagley of the British Museum of Road Transport, Coventry; the staff of the Francis Frith Collection, Andover; the reference department of Fareham Library; Alan King and his most helpful staff at the Local Studies Department of Portsmouth Central Library; Sarah Quail and the staff of the Portsmouth City Records Office; Alan Meaby and Brian Patterson of the Portsmouth Royal Dockyard Historical Society; and Alastair Penfold, Curator of Fareham Museum, are all deserving of thanks.

My good friends Russ Fox of Portsmouth City Museums; Geoff Salter of the Hampshire County Library Service; and fellow author Keith Smith whose railway knowledge is prodigious, also get my thanks.

And I must not forget my colleagues at *The News*, who are always so helpful. Thanks go to Brenda Wigmore, Dave Lolley, June Long and the staff of the photographic department, and Brenda Jacob and the staff of the reference library

Finally there is a debt of gratitude which is my greatest pleasure to acknowledge — that to my wife Sue, whose help and encouragement is ever present. Without her, none of my books would have been possible.

Anthony Triggs
Portchester
September 1992

I N T R O D U C T I O N

PHOTOGRAPHY has become commonplace. In fact a recent survey showed that it has now overtaken angling as Britain's most popular pastime. Nowadays almost every household possesses a camera, whether it is an inexpensive pocket camera, or a state-of-the-art single-lens reflex.

The very beginnings of photography actually go back to that period before Victoria came to the throne. By about 1800, Thomas Wedgwood, son of Josiah Wedgwood the Staffordshire potter, managed to produce what he called 'sun pictures'. White leather, coated in silver nitrate was placed in contact with such objects as leaves and was then exposed to the sun. The unprotected areas gradually darkened, leaving the shape of the objects white, rather like the mark of a watchstrap on a sunburnt arm. The only problem was that the image could only be viewed in a darkened room, for any sunlight would darken the rest of the leather, and the image would disappear.

About 25 years later, in France, Nicephore Niepce managed to record an image using a simple lens and an exposure of about eight hours. His extremely crude result is considered to be the earliest form of true photography.

Niepce's experiments caught the attention of another Frenchman, Louis Daguerre, who worked on a principle of producing images on a metal plate. Copper plates were coated with silver and rendered light-sensitive with iodine vapour. The exposed plate was 'developed' by holding it over heated mercury.

Victoria had been on the throne for a mere two years when Daguerre made his process public. He had come to an agreement with the French Government that in exchange for a pension, he would allow his invention to be used freely in France.

Daguerreotypes, as they became known, took the public fancy and the practice spread like wildfire. Soon, cameras and their cumbersome tripods were seen everywhere. Such was the popularity of the new craze that painters and artists became alarmed at the threat to their livelihoods, and the artist Paul Delaroche complained 'from today, painting is dead'.

At first the main disadvantage of the process was the excessive exposure time; sitters were expected to keep still for as long as 30 minutes. However, a new lens developed by Josef Petzval of Vienna, cut this time down to about a minute.

But Daguerreotypes were still a one-off process because there was no way to duplicate the image. This problem was to be solved by an Englishman, William Henry Fox-Talbot. Fox-Talbot was a wealthy landowner, MP., and amateur scientist, who had been working at his home at Lacock Abbey, Wiltshire, on sensitising writing paper to make a simple negative that could be contact printed. His process, the Calotype, was by no means perfect, but it did pave the way towards a method that was to revolutionise the burgeoning photographic world.

By 1851, Britain was at the height of her technical and scientific revolution, and various learned scientific papers were published in an effort to spread the word of progress. Out of this melting pot came news of experiments by an obscure London sculptor and photographer, Frederick Scott Archer. Like so many others he had been trying to improve picture taking by using glass plates, which would not show the grain as did Talbot's sensitive writing paper. Glass was the obvious answer, but the problem was how to get the emulsion to bind to the plate.

Archer had discovered that a sticky liquid called collodion — gun cotton dissolved in ether — formed a good binder, and from that the collodion process was born.

The system was also called the "wet-plate process" because the mixture had to be coated on to the plate, exposed in the camera, and developed while still wet. Although the process had many advantages — clarity of detail, unlimited prints, inexpensive production, and short exposure time — it nevertheless was a cumbersome and awkward business.

Photographers were obliged to take their darkrooms with them on photographic trips, often in purpose-built carts. For all this, the wet-plate era produced some of the finest photographers of the time.

The Isle of Wight housewife turned photographer, Julia Margaret Cameron, whose portraits of her influential and artistic friends were highly acclaimed, was one of this number. Roger Fenton, who took a horse-drawn darkroom wagon to the Crimean War, was another.

But a man who set himself a mammoth photographic task — to record every town and village in the country — was Francis Frith. Frith was a devout Quaker who set up a wholesale grocery business in Liverpool, which he sold at the age of 34 for almost £200,000. He had always been fascinated by photography, and now he was a rich man he could indulge his hobby, which he combined with his love of travel.

Between 1856 and 1860 he made three pioneering trips to the Middle East, taking with him a specially-designed wicker-work carriage which acted as camera, laboratory and sleeping quarters. He was also the first photographer to explore the dark continent of Africa, ten years before Livingstone and Stanley.

Upon his return to London he was given a rapturous welcome, and his reputation was made. He then altered course and set about the task of photographing every town and village in the country. For the next 30 years he travelled the country with his camera, and by 1890 had created the largest photographic company in the world.

After his death in 1898 his sons took over the family business, and the company continued to prosper as a postcard producer until well into this century. Today this priceless historical archive of nearly 350,000 views are carefully stored at the company's new headquarters, here in Hampshire, at Andover.

Although the picture quality was good, the inconvenience of collodion photography sparked research into a better binder for the emulsion that could be used dry. Various substances were suggested, but they all had drawbacks, such as greatly reducing the light sensitivity of the emulsion. Then in 1871 a Southampton doctor, Richard Leach Maddox, discovered that gelatine — as used in jellies — was what the photographic world had been seeking for the past 70 years.

The gelatine could be 'ripened' by heating before the plates were coated, which speeded up the sensitivity, and soon exposures of as little as 1/25th of a second were possible. The 'dry-plate' completely changed the face of photography.

But the real revolution came in 1880 when a 24-year-old American bank clerk, George Eastman, made and later patented, the first roll-film camera, using the now-famous Kodak trademark. Initially the user had to send the camera back to Eastman's factory, where the 100-frame film was developed and a new roll loaded into the camera before it was returned to the user. Eastman's slogan, 'You press the button, we do the rest' caught the public's imagination and the company went from strength to strength. Its founder became a multi-millionaire.

From these early beginnings the photographic industry as we know it today grew. The invention of 35 mm film, electronic flashguns, single-lens reflex cameras and now video camcorders have brought into common use what was once considered wicked alchemy. But still, the pictures taken when photography was young, are the objects that evoke the avid interest of local historians. For it is these pictures, gathered so laboriously and with such acute attention to detail that reflect not only changes in photographic technique, but the changes in the world in which we live, bringing into view scenes that can never be re-created.

NILE STREET, PORTSMOUTH, 1937. A jubilee or coronation is a sure reason for a cameraman to be out and about. The view was taken in 1937 and the street is decorated for the coronation of George VI, quite soon after the abdication of his brother Edward. Residents are out in the street to pose for the photographer and for they and their dwellings to be recorded for posterity, although they could never have known the changes that were in store. Nile Street which stood near the Unicorn Gate, and ran between Unicorn Road and Conway Street, was swallowed up in the massive redevelopment of the Flathouse area.

T O W N   L I F E

THE GROWTH of towns and cities in the past one-hundred-and-fifty years has had a profound effect on the lifestyle of the average Englishman. Many thousands gave up the country life to become town dwellers amid the smells, smoke, and dust of industry.

Cities and towns had grown rapidly since the Industrial Revolution, and so had the population of the British Isles. At the beginning of Victoria's reign, 11 million people lived in Britain. By the time her son Edward finally came to the throne there were 20 million.

The Victorian period was one in which England's influence on the world was at its greatest, and in which there was a significant change in society, with health reform, poor relief, and education much improved. At first the emerging towns and cities grew with scant regard for planning rules or design. Rows upon rows of tiny houses were built to house the new workforce, and within

Left : CROSS STREET, PORTSMOUTH, 1929. Children play in the street with the old stand-by — soap-box carts. Traffic was almost non-existent in the smaller streets of Portsea, so youngsters could play in relative safety. Other playtime favourites, for middle class children at least, were marbles, whip and top, and hoops — and each of these in their proper season. Children of less affluent parents — and there were many of them — would make their own enjoyment. Paper boats in the gutter water was a popular sport, and one that would be all but impossible to play today.

these areas there was little in the way of sanitation or waste disposal.

Local government did little to improve the living conditions on their doorsteps, often believing that things would change for the better on their own accord. Eventually municipal leaders began to realise this was not to be the case, and from 1870 local government began to play a more important role in local affairs than before, and huge ostentatious town halls were built to house the policy makers. Portsmouth's new town hall, now the Guildhall, was opened on August 9, 1890.

The original hall stood in the middle of High Street, Old Portsmouth, and became such an obstruction that it was removed in 1836. A new site was selected for it on the High Street, and the new building was opened in May, 1837. This building soon proved to be too small, and the site of the current Guildhall was acquired. Although considerably damaged in the war, the present Guildhall has been rebuilt to almost the same design.

For the ordinary person life was a squalid affair, with sickness and disease commonplace. Many children died in infancy, and many wives in childbirth. An outbreak of cholera hit Portsmouth in 1830, and again in 1848, when more than 1,000 people died before the disease had run its course.

Medical treatment was rudimentary, to say the least, until 1822 when a dispensary was set up in St. George's Square to

HIGH STREET, OLD PORTSMOUTH, 1875. *High Street was once the main artery of Old Portsmouth in those dignified Victorian days. The Dolphin Hotel is seen on the extreme right of the picture and just a little way up, above the roof of an adjoining building, is the sign for Monk's Oyster House. In the distance is the George Hotel where in September 1805, Nelson spent his last hours before embarking for Trafalgar. The room was preserved in its original condition, sadly to be lost when the building was destroyed during the Blitz.*

HIGH STREET, OLD PORTSMOUTH, 1924. The church of St. Thomas was elevated to a cathedral in 1927. It was founded in 1185, and became a parish church in 1320. The nave was rebuilt in the 17th Century, completely obliterating the original medieval nave. In the 1930s more extensions were planned — in a Romanesque style by Charles Nicholson — but the war intervened before the work was completed. The extensions are now going ahead, much of it thanks to public donations. After the church of St. Thomas became the cathedral, many of the old shops and houses were pulled down to form the grassed area now known as Cathedral Green. This picture — looking over the rooftops — shows the cathedral tower in the background.

provide eye and ear diagnosis for the poor. Later, in 1849, the Royal Portsmouth Hospital was opened, followed in 1874 by St. James's Hospital for the treatment of the mentally ill.

Robert Rawlinson, an inspector for the Board of Public Health, in an 1850 report to the General Board of Health on the Sewage, Drainage and Water Supply of Portsmouth wrote of Messum's Court in Old Portsmouth: "It is below sea level, is therefore very damp, and is reached through a tunnel only two feet wide. Here 116 people lived, some of them in cellars, with one privy between them and one standpipe which supplied water for perhaps ten minutes a day. Through the court ran a large open drain as well as an open midden, and when this was emptied the contents would remain for three days". Messum's Court lay between Prospect Row and St. Mary's Street, and was originally called Squeeze Gut Alley — for obvious reasons.

HAVANT 1935. This superb view of Havant was obviously taken from the tower of St. Faith's church and shows a little single-decker bus just about to leave for Hayling Island. Together with the photograph on the contents page (5) these two views, looking in opposite directions, show how little Havant had changed in the intervening years. In the more recent view (and the only business common to both photographs) is Davies the chemists with a veterinary branch next door, then the Dolphin Hotel, Home and Colonial Stores, Longs Cafe and finally the Central Garage. The panorama would have changed radically after the war when the new shopping precinct was built, leading from West Street up to the railway station. Today Havant is in the throes of change once more, as the new town centre redevelopment scheme takes shape, set as it is, to completely alter the face of Havant yet again.

Left : WEST STREET, FAREHAM, 1948. This view of West Street epitomises the days before parking meters and double yellow lines. Fareham market always meant big business and this picture was probably taken on market day when the more affluent shoppers could park their cars down the centre of the road. The white building in the distance is the Savoy Cinema which opened in 1933. A little further on is the Embassy Cinema which came a little later, in 1938, and opened with 'Doctor Syn' starring George Arliss.

In 1863 the Local Government Act gave the council more responsibility for public health, and slowly but surely improvements in the water supply and in drainage began to take effect.

However, even by the 1920s there were still many parts of Portsmouth still existing with squalid and dirty living conditions. The small passages which ran off Queen Street were particularly unsavoury, being packed with ale houses and brothels. There still was little or no drainage, and many of the wretched inhabitants — who lived in the one-up-one-down hovels — were forced to keep their refuse in their homes.

Eventually it was the murder of a pitiful prostitute — Brighton Mary — in Blossom Alley, and the resultant newspaper publicity that prompted the council into a huge improvement campaign. Much of the area was pulled down, and the town's first council homes were built in Curzon Howe Road.

The "Good Old Days" were invariably extremely hard. Portsmouth author Richard Esmond, who grew up in Orange Street, Portsea, wrote the following evocative piece about his boyhood at home in his book *Portsmouth Not So Old.*

"Bathrooms were not common in the old Portsea, but the big

This page : OYSTER STREET, PORTSMOUTH, 1935. Oyster Street ran from High Street, Old Portsmouth, to the Camber. In 1716 there were five inns listed in its tiny length — the Roebuck, the Crowne, the Bell, the Plume and Feathers, and the Baker's Arms. A few years ago, during an archaeological dig prior to redevelopment, the remains of a previously unknown part of the clay pipe industry was discovered in Oyster Street. The broken remains of more than 2,000 clay pipes were discovered, and upon futher excavations, the wall of the kiln and a large amount of pipe clay was brought to light. Up to then it had been thought that all the pipes for Portsea Island had been made at Portchester, so the discovery enabled museum experts to take a fresh look at the industry.

bathtub in the cellar was not a bad substitute", he wrote. "Many of the citizens of Greater Portsmouth, or their parents, originated in Portsea in its earlier days, and they are interested to remember it as it was before changing standards and bombs had their way."

"They will remember the closer-knit life of the smaller Portsmouth ; the little old houses that boasted no forecourts or front gardens ; the attics ; and the cellars which held the coal as well as the bathtub. Down there one went with bigger brother to bring up the coal, and sometimes singed his hair with the candle flame as he bent to shovel the coal, for one's eyes were fearfully searching the dark corners of the cellar, instead of attending to the candle."

The mode of dress changed very little. No one — man nor woman — was seen out without a hat. Flat caps for the workers, bowlers and waistcoats for the foremen, and silk toppers and frock coats for businessmen.

Women took a great pride in the headgear, with rich colours, feathers, and fruit, and even in later life when a bonnet was *de rigeur*, some of these were quite elaborate.

Previous page : EDINBURGH ROAD JUNCTION, PORTSMOUTH, 1900. A policeman helps two sailor-suited youngsters across the busy junction of Edinburgh Road and Commercial Road, while cyclists and horse-drawn vehicles trundle by. In the background can be seen the doorway of the Empire Palace theatre. The theatre opened on November 2, 1891, and was designed by opera house architect C J Phipps. In 1913 the theatre was completely renovated and renamed the Coliseum, with Marie Lloyd topping the bill on the grand reopening. After the second world war it was again refurbished and given back its old name. Sadly it eventually succumbed to the invasion of television and closed in September 1958. A supermarket was later built on the site.

Casual clothing was almost unheard of. Women and girls wore long skirts right to the ground to prevent display of their ankles, while most boys wore knickerbockers until at least the age of 15 or 16. And both sexes wore boots — the boys' were hob-nailed, and the womens' lace-up.

Shopping too was so different from today. Commercial Road shops stayed open until 8 or 9-o'clock as a matter of course, and by the end of the evening it was like a Bank Holiday. People would just stroll about taking in the sights and sounds. There would be a few fist fights, but a smart cuff round the ear from a policeman would soon disperse the participants.

There was street entertainment both legal and illegal, and in the back streets cock-fighting and dog-fighting was staged until well into this century. The latter, sadly, seems to be making a comeback with the resultant publicity concerning the new strains of fighting dogs.

Lack of cash to pay for the shopping was always a problem, and the pawnbroker's shop often became the last resort. Watches, rings, clothing, almost anything would be delivered to "Uncle's" on a Monday morning, to be redeemed the following Friday when the wages were paid.

For the less well-off buying a Sunday joint could be a hit-or-miss affair. With no refrigeration, by late Saturday evening butchers would sell off their unsold meat cheaply. Unfortunately, if the husband had stayed too long in the pub and missed the butcher's bargains, then it would require a swift outing for the rolling pin when he eventually arrived home, meatless. The meal for a child could well have been just bread and dripping.

Shops in those days were almost all small businesses, with no sign of the huge multiples that were to surface in later years.

KINGSTON RD, PORTSMOUTH, 1938. This evocative view, from the tower of St. Mary's Church, shows a tangle of tiny houses and streets, so typical of the city at that time. Work is being carried out on the facade of the Museum Gardens pub. Next to it can be seen the upper windows of the Fratton Fire and Police Station. To the north, traffic is visible at the junction of Kingston Road and Lake Road, with the Tramways Arms public house on the corner. Much of the area disappeared with redevelopment, to be replaced by high-rise flats. Lake Road has been re-aligned and now enters Kingston Road opposite the nearest row of shops with white blinds.

Portsmouth eventually boasted one of the very first self-service stores in the country — the Co-operative Society grocery shop in Fratton Road. Most food was bought loose, and those then-familiar blue paper packets held anything from sugar to baking powder.

Milk was purchased as required from the milkman who carried a huge churn on his cart. It was measured out into whatever receptacle the customer could provide.

During the last war much of the face of Portsmouth and its environs was changed, with many streets virtually disappearing from the city map. Recent development however has done more to change the face of the city than German bombs ever did. Today, new fly-overs, trunk roads and motorways have cut huge swathes through what was once the proud Portmuthians' tiny piece of that green and pleasant land we call England.

This page : HIGHBURY STREET, PORTSMOUTH, 1937. This was the workshop and home of John Pounds, one of Portsmouth's most famous sons. Born into a poor family in 1766, Pounds was crippled in a dockyard accident while still very young. He later set up as a shoe repairer in this little weather-boarded house in what was then St. Mary's Street. He encouraged the poorest street urchins of Portsmouth to visit him, initially for food then later for his reading and writing lessons and for instruction in the arts of cobbling. Pounds, who died in 1839, was remembered for his good works and the Ragged Schools Movement grew out of this remembrance. Sadly the house was demolished with the construction of Portsmouth Power Station which in turn has also been demolished.

BRITAIN STREET, PORTSEA, 1929. Britain Street was situated just off St. George's Square, near the Mill Dam barracks. The flat-fronted houses, with their shallow bays, are typical of the period. It is interesting to note the Fareham-made chimney pots with their distinctive white bands. Britain Street has one claim to fame — in one of these little houses on 9 April, 1806 the great engineer, Isambard Kingdom Brunel, was born. Brunel's father, Marc, was the inventor of the block machinery in the Dockyard and the son displayed a similar inventive aptitude. He later designed Clifton Suspension Bridge, Saltash Bridge, the SS Great Western — the first regular liner between Britain and America — and SS Great Eastern, which boasted accommodation for 4,000 people. Brunel died on September 5, 1859.

Previous page : UNION STREET, PORTSMOUTH, 1929. Union Street ran between Kent Street and Queen Street and shows very clearly how the poorer parts of Portsmouth once looked. The tall chimney of what is obviously Brickwoods brewery buildings on the opposite side of Queen Street is seen in the background. In the early Thirties much of the area, including the adjacent White's Row, was demolished to make way for Portsmouth's first council houses. The murder of prostitute Brighton Mary in nearby Blossom Alley prompted a new look at the area, after vivid descriptions of the wretched woman's squalid lifestyle appeared in local newspapers. Many of the dark little alleyways were demolished and the first new homes — in Curzon Howe Road — were built.

ST. GEORGE'S SQUARE, PORTSEA. *The birthplace of Sir Walter Besant. Besant was born on August 14, 1836 and went to school in Southsea at St. Paul's, going on to graduate from Kings College, London. In collaboration with Edward Rice, Besant wrote many novels and stories. 'By Celia's Arbour' had its principle scenes set in Portsmouth and it contains many interesting descriptions of the old town. Besant died on June 9, 1901.*

DANIEL STREET, PORTSEA. *The home of Jeremiah and Charles Chubb, founders of the well-known lock-making company. Jeremiah was said to be the inventor of the revolutionary Detector Lock, which should have made his fortune. Sadly he could not stand the pressures of life and drifted into poverty, leaving the field open to his brother Charles to continue with the company, which soon became known all over the world.*

Left : COMMERCIAL ROAD, PORTSMOUTH.
*Lastly in this series of famous houses, here is one
that recalls the birthplace of one of Britain's
greatest novelists — Charles Dickens. Dickens was
born on February 7, 1812, at 1 Mile End Terrace,
Landport, which had been home to his family since
1809, though the address is now 393 Old
Commercial Road. By the summer of 1812 the
family had moved to less expensive accommodation
at 16 Hawke Street, Portsea, and later to Wish
Street in Southsea, returning eventually to London
in 1814 before moving to Chatham in Kent. After
various jobs the young Charles took to writing and
in 1834 his first piece of fiction was published. Just
two years later, when he was 24, the first of the
Pickwick Papers was published and Dickens's
reputation was assured. Dickens returned to the
town in 1858 and 1866, on the latter occasion he
located Mile End Terrace but was unable to
identify the actual house.*

DICKENS *in 1866, around the time of his second
visit to Portsmouth.*

NORTH END, PORTSMOUTH, 1937. On a deed of 1699 the area was described as 'the north end of Kingston' and eventually an abbreviation of this came into general use. The Southdown Bus Company offices in the centre of the picture replaced an earlier building named The Poplars. Removal firm White and Company have their warehouse on the corner of Stubbington Avenue, next to the Clarence public house, with the sign advertising Long's Ales and Stout on the wall. It is interesting to note the group of workmen in the centre of the junction. It is possible they are removing redundant tram lines, which can be seen running down the centre of London Road.

Above : THE HARD, PORTSMOUTH, 1890. *In the old days the area around The Hard was known as 'the Devil's Acre' because of the number of taverns and public houses. At one time there were 16 drinking establishments out of a total of 27 buildings. This area and Queen Street, the main thoroughfare leading to the centre of town, became infamous because of its slums, alleyways and brothels. Today The Hard is the gateway to Portsmouth's world famous maritime heritage area.*

Right : PORTSMOUTH TOWN STATION, 929. *This unusual view from from the top of the Guildhall portico (see page 28) shows the goods yard and the high-level platform. Horse-drawn wagons of various types inhabit the goods yard including one owned by Pickfords. Away in the middle distance is the old fish market. This area now has been swallowed up in the civic offices development. The station itself of course remains but even that has succumbed to modern refurbishment.*

Far left : THE GUILDHALL, PORTSMOUTH, 1935. In 1880 the Portsmouth Corporation acquired from the Government a site which was once the official residence of the Commanding Officer of the Portsmouth Garrison, previously the residence and brewhouse of Sir Thomas Ridge. On this parcel of land the new Town Hall, now the Guildhall, was constructed. The design was based on Bolton Guildhall, and the entire construction cost £139,000. The foundation stone was laid on October 14, 1886 by the Mayor, Mr. Alfred Blake and on August 9, 1890, the Prince and Princess of Wales officially declared the building open. The Bolton Guildhall, although slightly smaller, was said to have cost £170,000.

This page : THE GUILDHALL, PORTSMOUTH, 1941. This was the scene at Portsmouth Guildhall after the German bombs had devastated it on January 10, 1941, leaving only the outside walls standing. The heat from the fires was so intense that it was several weeks before it was possible to enter the gutted shell. Paintings, statues, and beautiful walnut panelling were all lost, as were many other civic treasures. However, the muniment room, deep below the tower, escaped the worst of the heat, and the archives and civic plate were found to be undamaged. The Guildhall was rebuilt and reopened by the Queen Elizabeth II on June 8, 1959.

Left : COMMERCIAL ROAD, PORTSMOUTH, 1938. A market trader unloads his wares outside the Classic Cinema. It is interesting to note the names from the past on the adjacent shops — Home and Colonial Stores and Weaver to Wearer and some names that persist today — H. Samuel and Bateman Optician. The Classic cinema (here showing Get off my foot) began life as Cinenews on September 14, 1936 and was renamed in 1937. It was unusual in that it was one of the few news theatres to have opened outside London and ran a continuous hourly performance of cartoons, comedies and news programmes. It eventually closed in August 1972 — its site now lost in the modern Commercial Road development.

Above : COMMERCIAL ROAD, PORTSMOUTH, 1945. The aftermath of war left a great difference to the skyline of Portsmouth, as this simple view shows. At this time residents were just beginning to rebuild their lives after a long period of austerity. The wide open space on the right of the picture was pre-war, the premises of Landport Drapery Bazaar. The building was reconstructed and eventually became Allders department store. The tiny road running away to the right is Arundel Street. In the background are some of the properties seen in detail on the facing page plus Burtons the tailors and Marks and Spencer — all more or less survived the Blitz, as did the ornate facade of Lloyds Bank on the extreme left.

Left : HANDLEY'S CORNER, SOUTHSEA, 1935. *Handleys department store decorated for the Silver Jubilee of George V and Queen Mary. Handley's Corner was not the position of just another store but a Southsea institution. It became the favourite meeting place of all who wished to be noticed. Founded in 1869 by George Handley it grew to become the city's most fashionable emporium. George Handley died in 1926 but the business was continued by his sons Douglas, George and Trevor. The store was bombed-out in the war. Today the store is part of the Debenhams empire.*

Above : HANDLEY'S CORNER, SOUTHSEA, 1947. *In this similar view, looking down Palmerston Road the new Handley's is just beginning to rise from the ashes. The ornate National and Provincial Bank of England building is boarded up and was eventually demolished. The shops on the other side of the road had been rebuilt and Boots the Chemist are already in residence. A comparison of the two photographs, which show that a policeman's duties were much the same, also shows how many fine buildings were lost to German bombs and post-war redevelopment*

Above : ELM GROVE, SOUTHSEA, 1880. Now just an ordinary shopping street, Elm Grove was originally called Wish Lane. The land on the north side consisted of small farms. Ballard's Fields extended from Green Road to the passage leading to Belmont Street. Then came Attweek's Farm, Newton's Farm and Wish Lane Farm, the last of which extended from St Peter's Grove to Victoria Road North. Elm Grove became a high-class residential area with large houses hidden behind the lines of beautiful elm trees after which it was named. When the houses were demolished to build the shops there was a huge public outcry but without response.

Top right : ELM GROVE, SOUTHSEA, 1931. History disappears from Portsmouth as the last elm trees are felled. There was public outcry at what was called the 'desecration' of the city but neverthless the trees still came down. There was still traces of snow on the trunks of the trees and the rooftops — for this was February and the South had just experienced a particularly hard winter.

Right : ELM GROVE, SOUTHSEA, 1935. An evocative view of this popular shopping thoroughfare in pre-war times. The bunting and flags are out to celebrate the Silver Jubilee of George V and Queen Mary. The carrier bicycles parked by the pavement indicate a far more leisurely pace, as do the small number of cars on the road. Boots' Elm Grove Pharmacy with its gold-coloured sign high up on the gable is seen on the right of the picture. In the background is the spire of Elm Grove Baptist Church.

Left : FRATTON ROAD, PORTSMOUTH, 1929. On July 22, 1929, the Lord Mayor of Portsmouth, Councillor J. Smith, opened the renovated and widened Fratton Road. From a narrow, greatly congested and dangerous thoroughfare, with only a single line of tramway for most of the way, it had been converted into a first-class, 50ft. wide road. All the houses and shops on the east side were set back in order for the work to take place. In the picture the civic procession can be seen in the distance, making its way steadily towards Fratton Bridge.

Above : TWYFORD AVENUE, PORTSMOUTH, 1953. This view along Twyford Avenue could have been taken at almost any time during the past 50 or 60 years, for in that time, as now, it would have changed very little. The trolley bus in the distance with the overhead power cables and the little car coming towards the camera could at first sight put the picture in the pre-war era, but the group of television aerials on the chimney just to the right of Meyrick Road puts the picture definitively in the Fifties.

42720. F.F & C°.

Above : THORNGATE HALL, GOSPORT, 1898. The old Market House on the beach at Gosport was constructed in 1812. It was the main market centre and courthouse for the town but later became the subject of much criticism, being considered unsuitable as a place of assembly. In 1884 a new centre, the Thorngate Hall, was opened, thanks mainly to the generosity of Gosport merchant William Thorngate. The Gothic style hall stood until the 1960s, when it was replaced by the Town Hall. The New Thorngate Halls, a community-centre complex, was erected later in Bury Road.

Right : GOSPORT FERRY TERMINUS, 192?. The kiosk for Gosport/Portsmouth ferry tickets proclaim the cost of the crossing to be one penny. However if you wished to travel between 5.30am and 9am, it was only half the cost — to cater for the dockyard workers, while at the same time a trip on a bus from here to Lee and back would cost 9d. Two ferries, with their rows of lifebelts, can be seen at the seaward end of the pontoon. In the background is a particularly good view of 1920s Portsmouth.

WATERLOOVILLE CROSSROADS, 1910. This view by Herbert Marshall, shows the Waterlooville crossroads from the opposite direction to the photograph on the half-title page (1). Portsdown and Horndean Light Railway tramcar No.6 looks for all the world as if it is going to run down the little white dog which is bravely crossing the tracks. The shop awnings, almost mandatory at the turn of the century, indicate that the view was taken in the summer although most of the women in the picture are wearing coats, and in one case a scarf. The pub on the left is a Gale's house, the Heroes of Waterloo.

Right : PEMBROKE ROAD, PORTSMOUTH, 1920. *This picture from between the wars shows the premises of the well-known firm of Charpentier & Co. Founded in the 1800s by W. H. Charpentier, who became famous for producing a succession of local guide books and directories. Later the company specialised in maps and local histories and in 1900 was responsible for publishing William George Gates' 'Illustrated History of Portsmouth', written to celebrate the centenary of The Hampshire Telegraph. Charpentiers' premises were destroyed in an air raid in 1941 and with them went an irreplaceable collection of illustrations of old Portsmouth.*

VILLAGE LIFE

AT THE BEGINING of Victoria's long reign much of the countryside was as it had been for the previous millennium. The Industrial Revolution had not spread too far into the Olde Merrie England of popular mis-conception, although certain aspects of farming certainly had changed during the Agrarian Revolution. Many millions of country folk had moved to the industrial towns and those left behind carried on with the age-old traditions.

The lords of the manors were still a force to be reckoned with, being judge, jury and employer at the same time and the gentry's working alliance with the Church made their position even more secure.

Originally the majority of villages were no more than isolated groups of cottages or houses and to many agricultural workers a trip of maybe five miles to the nearest town was an adventure.

Education was simple and many knew little more than the limitations that their own community dictated. The village school, with its handful of pupils and strict discipline, gave only a grounding in education and many young people soon left the confines of the classroom for the fields, working to bring in the crops to help support the family.

The majority of cottages were tied to the lord of the manor's estate and were leased or rented to farm labourers while they were in his employ. Sadly this system inevitably bought hardship to tenants who became too ill or too old to work. Later the more philanthropic landlords recognised the debt of gratitude they owed to long-standing employees and began to endow alms houses. However this was a long time coming and many families were split up when the breadwinner was unable to fulfil his or her tasks. The squire dominated village life and controlled the very existence of the inhabitants, in many cases it was little more than poorly paid serfdom.

Although there were many general farm labourers, there were also the craftsmen whose skills were an essential part of village life. Blacksmiths, weavers, wheelwrights, cobblers, gamekeepers and even snake and vermin catchers made an important contribution to the community. The gamekeeper had an especially onerous task, for poaching was rife and was considered a way of life for many poor families. In some cases families could not exist without the ability to subsidise their food with poached rabbit or even deer, though the consequences of being caught, transportation and the like, could be horrific.

The basic diet would have been root vegetables and some poultry or bacon if funds ran to it. Many families kept chickens, so eggs were often plentiful. Living conditions were certainly spartan by today's standards, with candle lighting, water from a well and only a small, smoky fire to heat a cold stone cottage. Summer life may have been idyllic but the cold winters must have brought terrible hardships. A few landowners allowed tenants to gather wood for the fire, but this was rare.

SOUTHWICK, 1929. *A pretty scene of old thatched cottages at Southwick. It probably represents most people's idea of a country village and the apparently idyllic life of the country dweller. The village is part of a large private estate and once was home to a priory which moved from Portchester in the middle of the 12th Century. Southwick House, built in 1841, is now part of HMS Dryad, the Naval School of Maritime Operations and has an earlier claim to fame when it was the Supreme Allied HQ at the time of the D-Day invasion. The village public house, The Golden Lion, like many small village inns, once had its own brew house, which ceased operation in 1956.*

In winter months a farm labourer could often find other work but in the south these jobs were few and far between. In his *Rural Rides* William Cobbett wrote: "Invariably I have observed the more purely a corn country, the more miserable the labourers".

Cobbett was the son of a Surrey farmer and always thought of himself as a yeoman by birth. He grew up to become a larger-than-life character and set himself up as a champion of anyone who suffered because of the corrupt actions of others. For a while he settled into farming and in 1805 purchased a property at Botley, a place he described as "the most delightful village in the world." Later he sold his cottage and rented Sherecroft House, near Botley Mill and a plaque opposite the mill records his time in the village.

The working day was governed by nature — up at dawn with work until the sun set. The women folk would stay at home and tend the house, garden and children, while the men would leave for the fields with their simple meal of bread and cheese wrapped in a handkerchief. Once a week the washing would be done in huge cauldrons of steaming water with blocks of hard, rough soap. Rubber gloves were many years in the future and raw, red, washday hands were commonplace.

In the evenings the men would invariably go to the village pub. In many small hamlets this was just an ordinary cottage where the tenant brewed his own beer and sold it in the evenings. The wife and daughter of the house would be the bar staff in this small enterprise. In Hampshire many small brewers started off in this way and became prosperous businesses as time went on.

The Beer Houses Act had been passed, which allowed anyone to pay a £2 fee and get a licence to sell beer from home. Spirit sales were not allowed and soon beer became the drink of the masses. The beer was served in jugs from the kitchen, which became known as the tap room and eventually other rooms, such as the lounge and the snug, were made available. And of course the beer was considerably stronger than the mass-produced fizzy pop we know today.

Because of the differing locations, villages took on their own separate physical identities. In woodland areas timber and thatch

Previous page : THE SHOE INN, EXTON, 1929. What is going on in the little Meon Valley village of Exton? Perhaps when the river overflowed an old bath chair proved to be the only way to travel without getting your feet wet! The Shoe Inn, in a more modern guise, still stands and with its riverside gardens it is a popular place to eat and drink in the summer. At this time Chichester brewers Henty and Constable, (an amalgam of G. S. Constable and Sons and Henty & Co.) were the landlord's tied supplier — their draymen are pausing from their work to join in the fun. The brick and flint construction of the building is typical of the area. The village has a medieval church, with a curious headstone in the graveyard depicting the Angel of Death summoning a student from his books.

Right : THE OLD VINE, WICKHAM ROAD 1928. The public house has always been a focal point for rural communities. This picture shows the landlord and landlady of The Old Vine, on the road between Wickham and Fareham. Then the inn stood alone — now the new premises stand amidst homes and farm buildings. The auctioneers' notice board with its plethora of farm and livestock sale posters, sets the scene for an agricultural way of life. Items being advertised for future auctions include 150 New Forest ponies at a Brockenhurst sale, the freehold of a 'workmen's club' at Stubbington, 50 'Hampshire Down Lambs' and 'Live and dead farm stock' at Teglease Farm near Hambledon and building plots at Thornhill near Bitterne and at Hedge End, Botley, Bishop's Waltham and Fareham.

were the thing, while in chalk downland areas such as Portsdown, flint and bricks were used. The chalk provided the lime for the cement, while local clay was highly recommended for brick making. The Fareham area provided a huge amount of building clay and the white-banded Fareham chimney pots were a distinctive feature of many thousands of houses.

As Victoria's reign progressed, conditions in the countryside declined. Imports of cheap food from abroad made farming a precarious business and many desperate farmers moved into the towns. Villages and village life decayed, especially in the south.

Then the policy of free trade began to hit home. Free trade had been tried at the end of the 18th Century with an agreement with France. However war broke out in 1793 and further steps towards free trade were not possible until after the end of the Napoleonic Wars in 1815. A strong free trade movement in Britain was directed and financed by manufacturers and merchants who tried to break the power of the landowners, so that food and raw materials might be imported more cheaply.

The law surrounding trade was extremely complicated, with no fewer than 1,500 statutes in operation. There was also the Navigation Acts which imposed duties on a huge list of articles carried in foreign ships. These laws were consolidated, import duties were lessened and soon Britain was exporting huge amounts of manufactured goods. But by the same token great amounts of imported foodstuffs, especially wheat, came in. Although the policy helped the north, with the mills and factories offering employment for all, the agricultural villages of the south suffered and as the century wore on the situation worsened.

Many country dwellers were forced to look to new horizons. Rather than go to work in Blake's "dark Satanic mills" they opted for a new life in the colonies. Australia, New Zealand and Canada beckoned and many millions emigrated, often helped by the assisted passage schemes, many of which were offered by landowners in the south.

In 1851 nearly a quarter of the population was employed in agriculture. These figures declined, until by 1914 the figure was just one tenth. As more emigrated, farmers were forced to turn to arable farming and eventually wages slowly began to rise as landowners struggled to retain an adequate workforce.

Even so, agricultural labourers were among the nation's poorest workers, especially in the purely agricultural counties of the south. Low wages led to low productivity and in *Lark Rise to Candleford* the author Flora Thompson, who lived for a while at Liphook, wrote of local labourers: "They detest nothing as much as being hurried".

Flora Thompson was born in Oxfordshire but moved to Liphook with her husband, a postmaster. She lived at the quarters next to the old post office, where she helped out behind the counter. The old post office is now a bank and the building in which she lived is identified with a plaque. There is also a bust of Flora at the front of the new post office.

Right : UPHAM, 1929. A idyllic scene in the tiny village of Upham, near Bishop's Waltham. Bicycling seems to be the best way to get to and from the village shop, which still stands today, although now it is a private house. The trees on the left of the picture have become more dense with the passing of the years, but all in all the village seems almost unchanged. In 1683 the poet Edward Young, the author of Night Thoughts, was born here. His father was the local vicar. At one time the industry in the area was making brushes and the public house, The Brushmakers Arms, bears witness to the skill.

Factories began to turn out agricultural machinery, cheaper than the local blacksmith could make it. Farmers hired the services of steam traction engines at harvest time, which did away with many of the horses and men employed by the old methods, reducing the skilled workforce even further.

The Death Duties law was introduced in 1894 and this hit the landed gentry right where it hurt — in the pocket. Many landowners left their homes to decay while they went into industry, both at home and abroad. Villages gradually fell into disrepair and many actually disappeared altogether.

In the early part of the 20th Century, with the development of the motor car, city dwellers decided to escape to the country whenever they could and this move brought some small comfort

This page : CHESAPEAKE MILL, WICKHAM, 1900. Visitors often query the name of the old water mill building just off the Square at Wickham. The site itself is ancient, but the present mill was rebuilt in 1820, as the datestone high above the doorway shows. During the American War of Independence, the British ship Shannon captured the American vessel Chesapeake outside Boston harbour — the first British success of the war. The Chesapeake returned as a British ship and eventually was sold to a breaker's yard at Portsmouth. Many houses in Portsmouth were constructed using Chesapeake wood and a large amount was bought by a Mr. Prior to rebuild the Wickham mill.

Right: CHESAPEAKE MILL, WICKHAM, 1937. This evocative picture shows the bags of grain on the sack floor of the mill. This floor was nearly always high enough for the sacks to be hoisted from the wagon below. The exterior view of the mill shows clearly the 'luccam', the wooden projection at the top of the mill building. This enabled the bags to be hoisted in one single lift through the loading door of the mill. From the sack floor the grain would work its way down the mill ending up as stone-ground flour, or in some cases, animal feed. The finished product was unloaded into the waiting cart by means of a hinged slide which folded up after use.

to the country people. Tea rooms, inns and cafes sprang up in every possible locality to cater for the hordes of trippers and the government saw the need for a better road network. The building and upgrading of these brought employment to many.

Between the wars, huge unspoilt country areas, such as the Lake District, Dartmoor and the New Forest, became the destination for many of the new tourists and as a result petrol stations and garages popped up even in the most remote areas.

Nowadays there is a renewed drive to return to country life. Town dwellers who can afford it, buy summer retreats in the country. Many millions of others commute to the cities from the country and the renting of cottages for summer holidays has brought a new-found prosperity. Indeed the invasion by the wealthy urbanites causes much resentment in the countryside where young couples are often unable to afford their own home and must move into the towns and cities to find accommodation.

Farming communities are being encouraged to diversify away from the land into tourism, other leisure businesses such as golf courses and by letting their redundant farm buildings for light industrial use. In a way country life has turned full circle, although today's country folk certainly do not have to endure the privations of 150 or even 75 years ago — life in the country is now a pleasure and much sought after by the town and city dwellers.

Right : KINCH'S FARM, CATHERINGTON, 1937. The farm, which has now disappeared, used a man-powered tread-wheel to raise water from the well. The well was thought to be 600 years old and it was certainly in use 200 years ago and continued in use until 1914. The wheel was 15ft in diameter and took 20 minutes to raise a 15 gallon cask up the 300 ft. shaft. Commonly known as a 'Great wheel', this type of wheel was used in medieval times not only for drawing water but for lifting stone and timber for large buildings. Often these wheels were situated in the roof and left there when construction was completed. The Catherington wheel can now be seen in the Weald and Downland Open-air Museum at East Dean in Sussex. Another example can be found in the village of Beauworth, near Bishop's Waltham.

BRIDGE STREET, WICKHAM 1932. A pleasant corner of Wickham, looking towards the church of St. Nicholas. The row of houses on the right of the picture is known as The Old Barracks and they are purported to have derived their name from their original use as officers' quarters. Even today a notice on the wall says: 'Notice is hereby given that all vagrants found in or near this place will be punished with the utmost severity the law will permit. By order of the Magistrates'. Opposite is Queens Lodge where Queen Anne is supposed to have stayed the night when it was a coaching inn.

Above left : THE GEORGE, COSHAM, 1930. The cutting at the top of Portsdown Hill was made in about 1800 and the debris carried down the southern slope to diminish the gradient through the village of Cosham. The result was that the level of the High Street was so raised that the roadway was as high, at least in some cases, as the bedroom windows of the cottages at its side. The last of these cottages disappeared in about 1900. Before the Napoleonic Wars the village consisted of just seven farmhouses and a few labourers' cottages with thatched roofs. Cosham was a convenient place to stop on the way into Portsmouth and as a result the coaching traffic grew and some of the farms were converted into hotels.

Above right : WICKHAM FAIR, 1946. This annual event in the little village of Wickham dates back to the time of Henry III, who granted it a charter in 1268. The first fair was held the following year, during the Feast of the Translation of St. Nicholas of Myra. One of the traditional features of the fair is the horse sales at The Star corner, where horse-trading families, many from the New Forest, gather to sell or barter their livestock. The sales begin with the traditional ceremony of 'wetting the horse's head' at the bar of The Star. Even today the fair is a popular event in the Hampshire calendar, when thousands of revellers and visitors fill the square. The steam powered 'gallopers' featured in this photograph were owned by the Stokes family. In the centre of this scene, almost in front of The King's Head Hotel, is a reminder of the recent war — a concrete bomb shelter for Wickham villagers.

MEON VALLEY, 1929. Picking watercress at the New Cheriton watercress beds. Cress has always been an important part of people's diet, because of the rich vitamin and iron content. Originally gipsies would gather cress from roadside ditches and sell it in the towns. Rail travel meant there was a large market available and large-scale growing was encouraged. Much of the Meon Valley was used where slow streams of even temperature were to be found. Often beds were created by laying faggots under clay and gravel until a solid surface was created. The cress was packed into cane baskets, called chips, each containing about 60 to 70 pounds weight of cress.

NORTH WALLINGTON, 1932. *This evocative picture shows the village of Wallington, just east of Fareham. The village was one of the early fording places on the Wallington River and archaeological finds have proved that human settlements have existed here since very early times. Wallington was famous for its tannery and its brewery. The former was established in the early 17th Century and the finished product was carried out by water from Fareham Quay. Later, when the railway arrived, Fareham Station became the point of departure. The brewery was a later addition to the village and its superior-quality ale was enjoyed until well into the 20th Century.*

GIPSY LIFE, HAVANT, 1935. It is so easy to picture the travelling folk as we so often see them today. However until well after the last war it was a different story. The gipsy families would make their itinerant way around the county with perhaps a small cart drawn by a pony or donkey, making a frugal living as they went. Some were tinkers mending pots and pans in the days when it was not easy for a housewife to afford a new one if the old one burned through. Many travellers gathered cress from the ditches to sell, and others cut trees and sold firewood and clothes pegs. This winter scene near Havant shows the gipsy life for what it really was — hard, dirty and cold.

CHIDDEN, 1902. This photograph by C. H. T. Marshall proved one of his most popular postcards and in his time he produced a number of different views of the area. This particular picture was taken near The Bat and Ball at Hambledon and shows the rural scene to its best advantage, as the farm workers allow their animals to cool off in the pond. The Bat and Ball is situated on Broadhalfpenny Down, well-known as the birthplace of English cricket and the inn carries some interesting cricketiana on its walls. The Hambledon team defeated England on 29 occasions from 1750 to 1787. A memorial was unveiled in September 1908, when the local team last defeated England.

Above : HORNDEAN, 1939. In the background can be seen the tower of Gale's Brewery, founded by farmer and landowner Richard Gale when he acquired The Ship and Bell Inn at Horndean in 1847. Now at least, some of his workers' pay would come back over the bar of the pub. The inn already had an established brewing business — as did many public houses — but Richard saw further potential. The company was registered in April 1888 in the name of Richard's son George — who was a man of 60 at the time — and hence it is his name that the company still carries and not that of the founder, his father. The company was registered under the new Companies Registration Act and is one of only 50 surviving from the first 1,000 registered.

Following page : HORNDEAN, 1929. Horndean village looks peaceful in this between-the-wars view. The war memorial — still standing today in a truncated form — looks bright and new. The little road to Blendworth can be seen in the centre of the picture. Merchistoun Hall, just south of the village, was once the home of Admiral Sir Charles Napier, who lived from 1786 to 1860. He is buried at the nearby 12th Century church of All Saints at Catherington. The church also has the family tomb of Charles Kean — son of Edmund Kean — and his wife, actress Ellen Terry, and his mother Mary, who lived at Keydell House.

LEIGH PARK, 1930. Forestry workers gather wood in the forests around Leigh Park House, before the area was given over as a housing estate for Portsmouth City Council. The old-style horse-drawn wagon shows clearly how the agricultural lifestyle had changed little until well after the Great War. The Leigh Park estate hand-over was masterminded by Portsmouth councillor Frederick Storey, who foresaw the need for council homes to house the ever-increasing population of Portsmouth and its catchment area, which itself was growing by the year. He arranged for the purchase of the land from landowner General Sir Frederick Fitz Wygram in a move which set the standard for council housing even up to the present. In 1901 Sir Frederick had received the Freedom of Portsmouth for his kindness in allowing the children of the town to use his estate as a holiday venue.

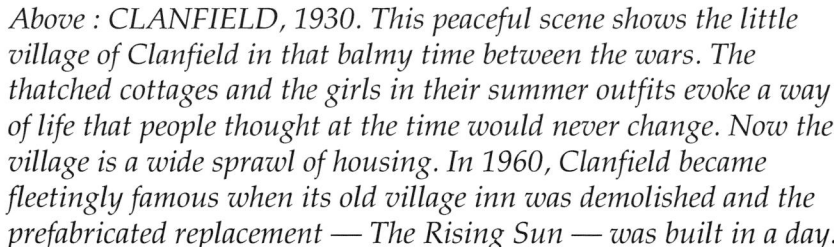

Above : CLANFIELD, 1930. This peaceful scene shows the little village of Clanfield in that balmy time between the wars. The thatched cottages and the girls in their summer outfits evoke a way of life that people thought at the time would never change. Now the village is a wide sprawl of housing. In 1960, Clanfield became fleetingly famous when its old village inn was demolished and the prefabricated replacement — The Rising Sun — was built in a day.

Above right : PURBROOK, 1937. The single line tram track runs through the little village of Purbrook, just south of Waterlooville. The wall alongside the grounds of Purbrook church with the school building just seen through the trees, was set back to widen the road some years later. The building with the white balustrade in the middle distance is the old Woodman public house, which was much used by labourers working on the construction of Fort Purbrook in the 1860s. The building was originally the lodge of the Purbrook Park Estate. The rebuilt Woodman is now situated slightly further south. Next to the church was Purbrook House, for many years the home of Captain Lynch-Staunton. It still stands but has now been converted into flats.

Left : LANGSTONE BRIDGE. HAYLING ISLAND. 1956. As with any island in the age of the internal combustion engine, vehicular access is of paramount importance. The original road bridge was opened in September 1824. The Duke of Norfolk performed the ceremony, accompanied by local dignitaries Sir George Staunton and William Padwick. As time went on and Hayling became a popular holiday resort for discerning visitors, there was just one topic of conversation — the toll. While it obviously deterred the 'masses' from invading the genteel resort it also became a needless barrier to increased trade for local businessmen and an extra cost for local residents. By the Twenties and Thirties, a toll was considered to be a relic of the past. The picture shows final stages of the construction of the present bridge, which was completed in 1956.

Previous page : LANGSTONE BRIDGE, HAYLING ISLAND, 1920. This superb aerial picture shows the view across Langstone Bridge in that quiet time between the wars. The railway line which carried the Hayling Billy and thousands of holidaymakers to the Island, can be seen running almost parallel to the old wooden road bridge. Eventually, by the early Fifties, weight restrictions meant the buses could no longer cross the old bridge and had to decant their passengers at the bridge for a brisk walk across to pick up another bus on the island. The toll house is situated on the road and is visible just above the motor bus which is travelling towards Havant. In the background this part of north Hayling looks very different to that of today, with only open fields and hedgerows to be seen. The last trains to Hayling ran on Sunday, 3 November, 1963.

PORCHESTER. — *The Village Street.* — LL.

Left : WEST STREET, PORTCHESTER, 1937. Although the basic shape of this row of shops in West Street remains similar, this part of the road is now a pedestrian precinct. West Street was once the main route for the A27 from Portsmouth to Fareham, but the modern by-pass now frees that part of the village from traffic chaos. Between the old road and the by-pass a modern health centre and library have been built, to serve the residents of the expanding village.

Below : PORTCHESTER FIRE BRIGADE, 1930s. The Portchester brigade was one of Hampshire's finest small, 'retained' brigades. It started out in the Twenties with a hand cart and later progressed to a motor-cycle and sidecar which towed the hand cart. Later the parish council purchased a 'Bullnose' Morris, two-seater car. This speeded things up, but the crew still had to hang on to the cart behind them. The Morris was later sold, a lorry chassis was purchased and the firemen converted it themselves into a 'proper' fire engine, complete with bell and brass handles.

Previous page : PORTCHESTER, 1910. All eyes to the camera in this evocative view of Castle Street early in the century. The baby in the bassinette is a particularly colourful touch. The cameraman has the castle to his back and is looking up towards the present-day shopping precinct. The New Inn, run by Ernest J. U. Ball, on the left, started life as a public house, but later became a village tea shop called The Ivy Rooms. This name was derived from the luxuriant growth of the climber which almost completely covered the building. The plant eventually penetrated the walls, which were three feet thick, and it became such an attraction that visitors and artists would travel from the Continent to see it.

Above : PORTCHESTER CASTLE, 1934. A popular summer day-out for Portsmouth folk was, and still is, a visit to Portchester Castle. The trees that once stood in the castle grounds can be seen through the archway. The building outside the gate to the left was the custodian's quarters, dating from the time of the Napoleonic Wars — 1786-1818. During this period between 3,000 and 8,000 prisoners were incarcerated within the walls, which necessitated up to 2,000 guards to oversee them. This eventually led to an upsurge in the number of inns in the area.

PORTCHESTER CASTLE, 1936. This superb aerial view of the ancient castle was taken between the wars. St Mary's — the church within the castle grounds — is clearly seen, although the line of trees from the church entrance to the land gate is now gone. In the graveyard of St Mary's, just discernible, is the grave of W. L. Wyllie, the celebrated naval artist who died in 1931. A lych-gate has now been added to the church and the foreshore has been built up into a proper sea defence. Portchester House stands alone in Hospital Lane to the right of the picture and the house on the foreshore at bottom right is now the headquarters of Portchester Sailing Club.

PORTSMOUTH DOCKYARD, 1904. *One of the most onerous tasks in the old-style navy, before the days of fuel oil, was coaling the ships' bunkers. This filthy process employed every member of a ship's company. The vessel's superstructure and guns were shrouded in canvas as a protection against the choking dust. Some of the older battleships held up to 3,000 tons of coal and when steaming at high speed they used up supplies at a prodigious rate. This rare dockside photograph shows bluejackets and Temperley's Transporter Haulabouts hard at work.*

W O R K I N G   L I F E

THE WORKING LIFE of the average working class Victorian was a pretty hard affair — long hours, poor working conditions, low pay and the constant threat of unemployment. There was no state safety net to catch the unfortunates who lost their jobs through ill-health or the decisions of ruthless employers.

Families were large and most parents were eager to get their children out to work and earning, even though wages were a mere pittance.

Young girls would often go into service, sometimes at the age of ten and by 1870 it was estimated that a third of the female population of England were working in service. Living conditions in this life of near slavery were poor, with attics or cellars provided as the minimum accommodation. In addition to the long working hours, many young girls had to endure the attentions of lecherous males in the household, who considered them fair game.

The inevitable outcome of this was that many young girls took to the streets. In 1864 the minister of the Kent Street Baptist Church told of the large numbers of young girls engaged in prostitution, many as young as 13 or 14.

Young boys fared little better and although those in the south did not have to face the horrors of the great mill factories or the mines, they nevertheless were put to work in extremely bad conditions. Breweries, tanneries, rope factories, and brickworks all needed young, cheap muscles to fetch, carry and lift.

Many children were taken on by itinerant workers, such as chimney sweeps, wherein they were forced to climb the chimney flues to loosen the accumulated soot and to guide the brush. Charles Kingsley in *The Water Babies* described the practice in all its terrible detail. This eventually helped to bring about the passing of the Factory Act of 1874, which brought the minimum working age to nine and the maximum working day down to ten hours.

Many youngsters chose to make a living on their own account. Some collected horse dung to sell to gardeners, others combed the sewers and many more sold matches. In a nation of smokers, matches were always a good seller and the match companies vied with each other to produce eye-catching and colourful labels to attract custom.

The invention of the typewriter in 1870, produced a whole new range of employment opportunities for women, but on the whole domestic servants were still in the majority — a situation which endured until the beginning of World War Two.

The new middle classes had the greatest effect on national life. These were the people who now went into business and commerce. Young men whose parents were upper middle class and had a little money, often went into the law, medicine, or the services.

Left : PORTSMOUTH DOCKYARD, *c 1904. Two bluejackets on coaling detail, lower a shipmate into the depths of the bunker to ensure even distribution of the load.*

Above : PORTSMOUTH HARBOUR, *1920s. Coaling of a different sort at the Camber as the S.S. Copsewood unloads on to the conveyor which lifted the fuel into the furnaces of the Portsmouth Electric Light Works. The generating station was built upon the site of the Highbury Street area, but now it too has disappeared under new housing development.*

PORTSMOUTH DOCKYARD, 1910. Navy stokers engaged on one of the other unpopular tasks. They are raking out the No. 2 boiler on an unknown vessel.

PORTSMOUTH HARBOUR, 1890. *A crowded corner of the harbour looking towards Portsmouth from the Gosport side. The top of the Semaphore Tower can be seen behind Victory. The two coaling tenders to the right have been named with the Russian royal family in mind — the Czarowitz and the Czarina. This picture from the Francis Frith Collection became an extremely popular postcard. Copies of all the Francis Frith photographs used in this book and many more, are available by post from this great national treasure house. The collection is of course based in Hampshire at Charlton Road, Andover, Hants. SP10 3LE.*

Other less privileged young men went into banking, insurance, or trade, but even those were not easy to enter. Having a friend already in the industry was a must. After a stringent interview, the successful candidate would be taken on to undertake some menial office job, where an ambitious youth could look forward to a long apprenticeship with a little hope of early promotion.

In Portsmouth the Dockyard and its ancillary industries were the big employer. In 1867, there were 5,628 men employed there, in addition to a large number of civil servants and Naval officers. By the turn of the century the workforce had risen to 10,439. These men were a new breed of worker — the artisans. Craftsmen such as ropemakers, blacksmiths and carpenters took on a whole new identity. Outside the 'Yard', with the huge sprawl of houses growing by the month, a veritable army of bricklayers, plasterers, plumbers, gas fitters and general labourers lived off the general prosperity of the area.

It must be remembered that Portsmouth was a garrison town — confined within its handsome fortifications — and the preponderance of service personnel led to many satellite industries. Three of the most important of these were the baking and brewing industries and the manufacture of uniforms.

The business of supplying food to the fleet goes back to the very birth of the Navy. There were bakehouses in Portsmouth in Elizabethan times and one was set up in King Street in 1724, which produced 34 hundredweight of ships' biscuits a week. The story goes that the bakers bought pigs which they fattened free of charge on their employers' biscuits. This fraudulent use of government property was not discovered until 1828, which in part led to the removal of the bakehouses to the Royal Clarence Yard at Gosport. The road leading to the yard was called Weevil Lane. This is said to have some bearing on the fact that the old salts would say that when eating ships' biscuits in near darkness below decks, it was sensible practice to strike the biscuit on the mess table to shake out the weevils.

There were other bakeries producing food for commercial purposes —Smith and Vosper in Southsea and William Miller, later to become Campions, in the town.

Flour milling was naturally an important supplier to the bread industry, and Portsmouth was well served by mills, the biggest and most well-known being the Dock Mill at Napier Road in Southsea. The mill was demolished in 1923 but the mill workers' cottages still remain.

The other basic necessity for the men of the fleet was well served by the breweries of the town. In the early 1800s there were as many as 40 in Portsmouth alone, but as in today's world they were gradually taken over by the larger concerns. Some of the names of the past which were swallowed up by Brickwoods were Longs, Portsmouth United Brewers, Pike Spicer and Bransbury's.

Brickwoods started off in a small way, but grew to be the largest brewer in the area. In 1851, Fanny Brickwood bought the Cobden Arms, a small public house and brewery in Arundel Street. Her grandsons Arthur and John carried on the business after her death and began a programme of expansion which was to continue until as late as 1953. Brickwoods was probably the best known local brewery until it in turn was eventually absorbed into the Whitbread empire.

Clothing the fleet and providing a seductive shape for women, were other industries to flourish in the town, and as early as 1800 there were a number a naval tailors in Portsmouth. One company with a name still apparent today — Gieves — was effectively started in 1785 by the grandfather of George Meredith, the poet.

Over the years the firm merged with others to form the company of today.

Until quite recently a walk down Queen Street would have provided a veritable directory of naval tailors, but with the depletion of the fleet, many of these have now disappeared.

The other important business — both for women and largely employing women — was the corset and dress industry.

Naval disasters at sea often proved to be a disaster at home with a widow left with a family and no income. It was from these needs

Left : PORTSMOUTH DOCKYARD, 1880. H. M. S. Jumna is pictured moored at Portsmouth Dockyard. The crew are manning the rigging as the Royal Yacht, Victoria and Albert, comes alongside, just below the Jumna's stern. Aboard the yacht was the Prince of Wales, later Edward VII, who was returning from an official visit. Jumna was one of five rig-and-screw troopships commissioned jointly by the Admiralty and the Indian Government. The other four were Serapis, Crocodile, Euphrates and Malabar, and all five were familiar sights in Portsmouth Harbour. In 1932 when Portsmouth became a city, the bow emblem, the Star of India with the motto 'Heaven's Light our Guide', was adopted for the municipal crest.

This page : PORTSMOUTH HARBOUR, 1900. The Royal Navy has provided a way of life for many Portsmouth men. In the old days, going to sea meant years rather than months and homecomings were to be savoured. Here, a superb study by Southsea photographer Stephen Cribb, shows a typical welcome at the quayside. However there is an astute pencilled note on the back of the original photograph written by Cribb himself. It reads: 'So near but yet so far. An officer having a few words with his wife, or somebody else's, as the ship comes alongside.'

PORTSMOUTH HARBOUR, 1909.With fresh bread only provided for officers the bumboat men and women would come alongside with meat and bread for the crews. Spirits were banned, but many wily bumboat owners often tried to beat the system. One woman filled pigs' bladders with spirit and smuggled them aboard a warship by hiding them beneath her skirts. On departure the skins were blown up to give her the same look she had on arrival. Blustery weather and an unfortunate capsize revealed her bloomers and the ruse to the watch officer.

that the early businessmen farmed out piece work dressmaking to be done at home. Often the whole family would be involved in the processes, working very long hours with little to show at the end of it. Making shirts — mostly for naval ratings — was the biggest part of outwork and indeed shirtmaking was still being carried on in the city until very recently.

By the middle of the 1800s there were a number of factories turning out stays and corsets and many patents were taken out to protect manufacturers' designs.

Eventually as whalebone stays disappeared and the glamorous, less supportive underwear of today began to arrive, the factories changed their processes to cope with the new fashions. In the post-war period some of the most famous labels in the lingerie world were produced in the city.

There were many other industries which were to have an effect on the area. Ropemaking, aircraft construction on the Portsmouth airport site, brickmaking at Burrfields, Southsea and Fareham, furniture making, tanning at Wallington, paint production and coachbuilding have all had a bearing on the workforce of the area, vying with the shipbuilding and fitting out talents of the Dockyard workforce.

Conditions certainly have changed, with the growing awareness of workers and the help provided by trades unions to promote better and cleaner working places, shorter hours and longer holidays. With industrial tribunals, unfair dismissal is almost a thing of the past — a far cry from the days when a child of ten could pay for a misdemeanour with the same severity as the punishment meted out to an adult. ❦

PITT STREET GATE, DOCKYARD, 1931. It's out-muster at the Dockyard, and workers are pictured leaving by way of the new Pitt Street Gate, which was opened along with the new East Gate in the early 1930s. Both introduced to relieve the pressure on other Portsmouth roads, when all workers left the yard by either the Main Gate or the Marlborough Gate. A newspaper seller waits to catch some trade.

DOCKYARD WORKERS, UNICORN GATE. *Not all Dockyard workers were of the two-legged variety — horses played a large part in getting the daily tasks done. This picture shows a number of Dockyard Clydesdales being led away on a warm Friday evening, in the August of 1933. These beasts of burden were used regularly until well after the war to undertake heavy pulling and heaving jobs in the 'Yard'. It was a hard life, but they did at least get their breaks at week-ends.*

Left : SPRING GARDENS, PORTSMOUTH, c.1935. The corporation stables were situated just off Spring Gardens in the Guildhall Square. They were built in 1877 and catered for all the working horses owned by the corporation including the fire brigade and the city engineers department as featured in the other photograph on this page. The fire brigade also had their station at the front of the block. Advertising billboards, to the right of the stable block, advise that you should always demand OXO for 'general fitness' and that 'beer is best'.

Right : PORTSMOUTH DUSTCART, 1939. The faithful horse stands patiently with his master for the photographer while the new City of Portsmouth dust cart is recorded for posterity. The leather tack and brass buckles have apparently received special attention before the driver set out for his appointment with the photographer. The dustman himself, wearing a flat cap and leather jerkin and with his trouser legs and sack apron tied up with string, is fairly typical of the working man of the period. Horses were much used by the corporation and their own stables were an important part of civic operations. The advice to 'burn your waste paper & litter' would not be endorsed by city authorities today.

Left : *BURRFIELDS BRICK FIELDS, PORTSMOUTH, 1925. Brickmaking was quite a business in the Portsmouth area and here workmen are pictured at the Burrfields site earlier this century. The site was opened in 1890 and the bricks were used for such local buildings as the Queen's Hotel and the officers' mess at H. M. S. Nelson. The raw material was dug on site and the bricks were baked on the spot. The labourer was paid for each cubic yard of clay he dug and the rate for actually making the bricks was, at that time, 5s. 9d. per 1,000. Boys were employed on the site in various jobs — as flatters, who helped shape the bricks, a pug boy, who carried the raw clay, and a page boy, who loaded the finished bricks on to the wheelbarrow. The road names around this area reflect the industry with Claybank Road and Kiln Road.*

HILSEA LINES, 1900. In 1860, with the threat of possible invasion hanging over Portsmouth, the old bridge from the mainland — which had not been strengthened since the time of the Civil War — was demolished and a new bridge and fortifications — the Hilsea Lines — were built. The fortifications were part of the group of defences against the French known later as Palmerston's Follies. There were the Solent forts and those on Portsdown. At that time Portsbridge was the only road on to the island and was of great strategic importance. In the Twenties much of the fortifications were demolished to make way for new road development. The new Portsbridge was opened in 1927, allowing the ever-increasing flow of traffic easier access to Portsea Island.

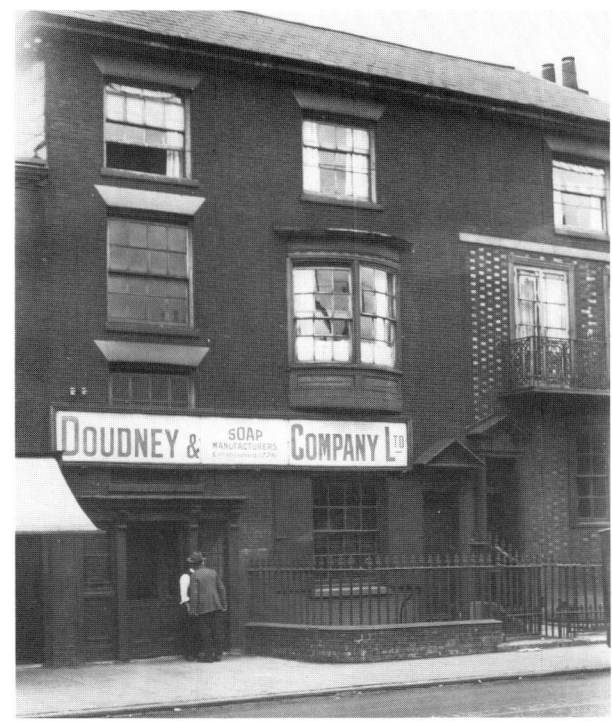

This page left and below : DOUDNEY'S SOAP WORKS, PORTSMOUTH, 1932. John Doudney started his business as a tallow chandler in 1776. After his death in 1834, the business was carried on by his sons George Ebenezer and Edward Phillip, who installed the new steam-powered machinery to take the tallow business a step further into candle production. The business was situated at 333 Commercial Road, Mile End, but by the end of the century the brothers had acquired the two next-door properties, nos 335 and 337. They also turned their attentions to soap manufacture and the company's 'Dolphin' brand became a popular seller. The picture below shows one of the firm's horse-drawn vans crossing the Guildhall Square in about 1905. The business closed in about 1930 and eventually the premises were demolished. There was another soap-making company, Tilleys, situated in Prospect Row, near the Gunwharf Gate.

Left : GOLDSMITH AVENUE, 1909. Tramway track is being laid along Goldsmith Avenue for the Milton extension. This scene was taken from an upper window of the Talbot Hotel. Work on the extension started on 18 March, 1909 and was finished by 30 June, but the line lay idle for three weeks to allow the concrete to set. The original estimate was £14,407, but in the event it cost £11,841. A decorated tram left the Town Hall at noon on 20 July, filled with members of the corporation. When the car reached Fratton Bridge, the mayor, James Baggs, took over as driver. The smooth running of the car was noticeable as this section was the first to have welded joints on the rails.

Above : LONDON ROAD, WATERLOOVILLE 1902. A gang of the workmen who were laying the tracks for the Portsmouth and Horndean Light Railway are pictured here outside the Wellington Inn. The foreman stands at the left with his Albert watch and chain tucked into his waistcoat. The landlord of the Wellington was Mr. H. E. Sly, and the entrance to the public bar was on the left, while the door on the right led to the bottle and jug, which many of the workers would have used during the construction of the railway. A jug of beer no doubt came as a welcome change from digging. To left and right are the horse drawn buses that the Light Railway would have superseded, at least in part.

Right : STEAMING AHEAD 1932. Waterlooville haulage contractor Harry Edney is pictured with one of his two Super Sentinel steam waggons, which he and his brother Ernest used to fulfil their 12-year contract to haul 15-ton loads of beer from London to Portsmouth. The brothers had to paint the name of the stout makers, Hammerton, on the sides of their vehicles. Both brothers declined to stay in their father's farming business, so each was given £1,000 and told to go it alone. They invested their cash in the haulage business, which became a success and were able to purchase the brand new steam waggons from the Sentinel works at Shrewsbury. One was bought in July 1929 and another in the December.

Left : WATERLOOVILLE, 1902. The first nine cars destined for the Portsmouth and Horndean Light Railway were delivered by train to Cosham station, off-loaded and then towed in threes to the Cowplain depot using a traction engine which pulled them along the newly-laid track. Once they arrived at Cowplain, local craftsmen undertook all the interior decor, fittings and seating. This picture, taken by C. H. T. Marshall, shows the convoy as it stops for a break in London Road, Waterlooville, conveniently adjacent to Marshall's photographic studio. The vehicles were ordered from the British Electric Car Company and each had a seating capacity of 54. They were painted in a livery of green and cream. The tramway eventually proved so popular that within a month a further five cars were ordered.

HAVANT, 1932. Th⌐ ancient craft of charcoal burning is ⌐ing practised here as the burner adjusts th⌐ air flow into the huge metal kiln. Bur⌐ing charcoal is probably one of Brit⌐'s oldest industries, for it was perfecte⌐ ⌐n before the Romans came to the⌐ shores. In the olden days the bundles of ⌐ood — usually oak and elm — were pil⌐ up in large conical heaps and covere⌐ ⌐h damp turf and leaves to produce ⌐ s⌐w but intense heat, which had to burn f⌐ four or five days. Later the metal ki⌐ns ⌐peeded up the process. The indust⌐ had declined considerably by th⌐ ⌐irties but had a brief upsurge during the ⌐r when charcoal was required for the ⌐oduction of 40 million gas masks.

Above : CLAY PIPE FACTORY, PORTCHESTER, 1935. Leigh & Company's clay pipe factory was established in 1840 and at its premises at the top of Castle Street it manufactured putty, whiting, hearthbricks and of course clay pipes. The clay was brought in to the quay at Paulsgrove from Cornwall and the company employed itinerant labour to mould the pipes at 8d.(c.3·5p) a gross. A pipemaker's gross was 16 dozen (192 pipes), to allow for breakages. This man is trimming the pipes before they are put in the kiln for firing. It is interesting to note this man's little work area, with its clock and the calendar and the paraffin lamp with a tin reflector. In its hey-day the factory was turning out 16,000 pipes a week and in addition to the familiar 'churchwarden' pipes they made others with names such as 'long straws', 'cutties', 'bulldogs' and 'Irish clays'. The latter, rather misleadingly, often had 'Dublin' impressed on the stems!

Below : PARCHMENT YARD, HAVANT, 1936. Parchment-making went on at Havant for over 1,000 years. Havant parchment was recognised as the finest in the world, mainly because of the special qualities of the water from Homewell spring, which produced the required whiteness. The raw material was sheepskin, but with the growth of frozen meat imports and competition from synthetic materials, the business declined and ended in 1936. These are the lime pits, or pokes, where skins were transferred from pit to pit, each containing a different strength solution. The site is remembered today only by the names of the side-streets, The Parchment and Homewell.

Above : UNEMPLOYED FELLOWSHIP CENTRE, PORTSMOUTH, 1932. Although this chapter is concerned with people making a living it is only fair to show the other side of the coin. The depression years of the late Twenties and early Thirties hit many millions around the country. Especially hard-hit in Portsmouth were the unskilled workers of the Dockyard — their chances of becoming re-employed quickly, would have been quite slim. The Unemployment Fellowship Centre was often refered to as the Inn of Good Fellowship as it was housed in a former pub in Commercial Road, Portsmouth, and just like a pub, it became a focal point for many local men. A hot cuppa, a game of cribbage or dominoes, a stove on which to warm the hands and a reading room to keep the mind active, were all considered beneficial to the unfortunate jobless of the area. It is interesting to note the map of Canada on the wall — a sign of the desperation which drew men and women to consider emigration to distant lands and uncertain futures.

PIER ROAD, SOUTHSEA 1900. The trams gather in the August sun as the crowds flock to 'Lord' John Sanger's circus. On Monday, 11 August, a strong wind was blowing along the seafront and the circus proprietors decided to end the afternoon show in case of an accident. The 2,000 seater big top was evacuated, but a little after five-o-clock a fierce squall suddenly developed and the whole big top blew up like a balloon and collapsed, the poles tearing the canvas to pieces. It fell on a number of people outside and some were badly injured. Two young boys were severely hurt and one, George Lee aged 14, died soon afterwards. Sanger was not in fact a real lord. His 'elevation to the peerage' came in 1887 when he was being sued in court by 'Buffalo' Bill Cody. Throughout the trial the American was correctly referred to as 'the honorable William Cody,' a title accorded to him as a member of the Nebraska legislature. Sanger was said to have growled 'If he's an Honorable, then I'm a Lord'.

RELAXATION

TODAY THE PURSUIT of leisure and pleasure is all important. The large number of country parks, theme parks, picnic areas and viewpoints bear witness to the Englishman's desire to get away from the daily routine and enjoy himself. The number of advertisements in newspapers for clubs, pubs, theatres and cinemas show that there is an almost endless variety of things to do and see. And with the working week becoming shorter, the average family has far more time to devote to rest and play.

But in early Victorian times the premise that one could actually enjoy leisure time was viewed with suspicion. Basically there were just the two classes of society. The moneyed class whose aim was to make even more money — and the working class who simply toiled for many hours just to make enough to survive on. The middle class had yet to surface.

Some of the more wealthy families undertook to emulate the late 18th-Century Romantic Movement, where poets, authors and artists began to explore the more wilder and unspoiled parts of the country in order to commune with nature. The nouveau Romantics of the 19th Century took their wives and children to such places as Dartmoor, the Lake District and the Scottish Highlands, but these trips were hardly leisure and certainly not pleasure.

Townspeople had very little to occupy them, and drinking — usually rough gin at a penny a glass — was their only respite from work. Gin drinking was so rife that many temperance societies —

such as the Rechabites — were formed with the express purpose of luring people away from the gin palaces.

One outstanding member of the Leicester Temperance Society was a man named Thomas Cook, who organised rail trips for workers to the country, as an alternative to them spending their time drinking. They were a great success, and from lowly beginnings he became the leader of the travel business throughout the world. The expression 'a Cook's tour' went into the language.

Cook organised trips to London and to seaside resorts — and when the Great Exhibition opened in Hyde Park in 1851, Cook transported a total of 140,000 workers from the industrial North and Midlands to see the wonders of the British Empire.

The exhibition was a showcase for the might and strength of the Empire and was dominated by the Crystal Palace — the massive glass and steel structure designed by Joseph Paxton especially for the show. Paxton was a director of the Midland Railway and was M. P. for Coventry in 1854. He was knighted for his services to the country and died in 1865. After the exhibition the palace was moved to Sydenham where it continued to attract thousands of visitors. Sadly it was destroyed by fire in 1936.

Trips to the seaside were steadily becoming an alternative to the inland spas. Many children had never even seen the sea and

NAVY DAYS, 1935. 'See the Ships and Meet the Men' was the slogan of Navy Days, held each year at major Naval bases around the country. Portsmouth was always popular and in their hey-day the open days pulled in huge crowds. The queues to enter the Dockyard often stretched far up Queen Street and inside the base there was always a long wait to go aboard the various ships. The bands played and there was continuous entertainment in the arena, with small-arms displays, drill and often the odd bit of slapstick. Here an expectant crowd awaits the start of the afternoon show. In the background is H. M. S. Nelson, flagship of the Home Fleet from 1927 until 1941

PORTSMOUTH DOCKYARD, 1932. Nelson's flagship HMS Victory was laid down in 1759 and launched in 1765. After sterling service of 157 years she was brought to her present resting place in dry dock in 1922. After a further six years of painstaking renovation work, she was finally brought back to her condition as at Trafalgar. On July 17, 1924 George V toured the old ship and his visit officially marked the completion of the mammoth task. Since then more recent renovation programmes have sought to consolidate much of that early work and ensure that Victory remains the centrepiece of the Navy's contribution to the heritage area.

SOUTHSEA, 1921. South Parade Pier, captured by one of the many Francis Frith staff photographers. Frith himself, who created the largest photographic company in the world, died in 1898, but his sons Cyril and Eustace continued his commercially lucrative, and in historical terms vitally important, quest to photograph every town in the country. This photograph shows the promenade with holidaymakers out taking the air. An elderly, bearded gentleman is pulling a bath chair and a cyclist parks his bike on the beach, while a brave young thing risks damage to her shoes from the pebbly shore.

donkey rides on the sands and Punch and Judy shows were a requisite part of a day at the seaside. As more people sought the sea breezes, the coastal resorts gradually prospered. The Southsea area — which originally consisted of Naval Officers' homes — became transformed into a high-class watering place.

An early Charpentier *Guide book for Southsea and Portsmouth* (note the predominance of Southsea) described the resort in glowing terms.

"Southsea is yet young as seaside resorts go," it read. "Year by year she is adding to her delights, and thus her fame is spreading. Variety is here in abundance; of sunshine there is a plentitude; for children there are joys unlimited. Here are scenes of might and vigour at sea ; here are quiet gardens and many resting places."

"So, from the shores of the grand harbour, into and from which sail her majesty's ships, there runs for all who will tread its ways, a great unbroken esplanade, past sea and shop, past long gardens of colour and perfume, past tennis courts and bowling greens, and children's lakes and kindred pleasures."

To the average working person the seaside attracted them like a magnet. The lure of the sea and sun and myriad pleasures they could not enjoy at home was irresistible. The pierrot shows with their slightly risqué humour, fortune tellers and the sight of a young lady in a bathing costume were all pleasures to be savoured. Although all was usually covered, a telescope on the pier would often reveal a tantalising glimpse of a bare ankle or shoulder, or a hint of the outline of a female form in a wet swimming costume.

As the influx of summer visitors increased, then the entertainment on offer widened. Both Southsea Common and Clarence Pier boasted a bandstand and Sunday concerts were a popular afternoon's entertainment following church attendance in the morning. Steamer trips left from the pier to the Isle of Wight, westwards to Bournemouth and east to the Sussex coastal resorts.

South Parade Pier had the usual amusements — an end-of-the-pier show theatre and the typical penny-in-the-slot amusement arcade offering the chance to win a small trinket or experience the titillation of 'What the Butler Saw' — in fact more than enough for a typical Victorian day out.

However it wasn't only the seaside that drew the holidaymakers. The countryside also became a popular destination — picnic excursions were a favourite — with special excursion trains running to areas of special beauty, such as the New Forest, Snowdonia, or the Yorkshire Dales.

The vogue for health and fitness which took over in late-Victorian and early Edwardian times provided a huge growth in sporting pursuits. Swimming clubs, athletics societies, tennis clubs, bicycling societies and other similar gatherings often had long waiting lists for membership.

Once cycling became a practical and popular form of relaxation, clubs began to form and many had their own uniform. Soon a standard uniform emerged, based on that worn by the Cyclists' Touring Club, formed in 1878. The basic wear was light knickerbockers, high boots and a simple jacket. The uniforms were dark in colour so that dirt from the road would not show up. Inns and small hotels catered specially for CTC members.

Later still, men wore ordinary Norfolk jackets and breeches, but the burning question was what the women who dared to cycle should wear? Fashion decreed ankle-length dresses, five yards around the hem with lead shot to keep them in place, over

layers and layers of petticoats, tight corsets on the waist and an elaborate hat.

Even spectating at major sporting events became the in thing, with rail links making travel to the venues so much easier. Cricket, football and horse racing were frequented by great numbers of spectators. Portsmouth Football Club was founded in 1898 and nearby is Hambledon, always accepted as the birthplace of English cricket as we know it today.

The turf fraternity had nearby Goodwood, opened in 1802, but which came into particular prominence when it was regularly visited by the Prince of Wales, later Edward VII. He was invariably seen travelling to the course in his open carriage, which gave the ordinary people a rare chance of a glimpse of royalty.

Portsmouth supported the Sport of Kings when it opened its first racecourse, Portsmouth Park, at Farlington in 1891. The course extended for 230 acres and the grandstand held 5,000 seated punters. A railway station was opened at Farlington to cater for racegoers. The course eventually closed at the start of the First World War and the land was taken over by the War Department. After the hostilities it remained derelict until 1929

Left : PORTSMOUTH HARBOUR, 1890. Sightseeing trips around the harbour have always been popular. Victorian trippers would have seen the huge flagship Duke of Wellington moored majestically in the harbour. The 6,071-ton warship was launched at Pembroke Dock as HMS Windsor Castle on September 14, 1852 — the day on which the Duke of Wellington died — and later renamed in his honour. At the time she was the largest vessel ever built in the world. She entered service at Portsmouth in May 1863 and was decommissioned in April 1904. As a comparison, Victory displaces a mere 2,164 tons.

when it was finally sold.

In 1928 a second attempt to bring racing to Portsmouth was made by local businessman George Cooper, who opened a course at Wymering. Here there was accommodation for 8,000 spectators and to cater for the modern age there was parking for 2,000 cars. A purpose-built railway halt was constructed for the projected influx of visitors. The course flourished until the last war, when it closed on 17 February 1938, and the land sold for building.

Golf became popular with both sexes and Southsea's municipal course was a great draw for holidaymakers, with a special season ticket for visitors.

The countryside also provided a wealth of material to satisfy the growing interest in flora and fauna. Butterflies, plants (especially ferns) and insects were all keenly pursued by enthusiasts, while amateur artists would sit and record the wildlife on canvas and sketch-pad.

Indoor entertainment improved in quality and quantity as patrons demanded better standards. The theatres—of which Portsmouth boasted a fair number — began as converted back rooms in pubs, but eventually they became purpose-built, until by the end of the last century they were opulent palaces of variety. The Kings Theatre and the Theatre Royal — both designed by Frank Matcham — are legacies of this great tradition.

When moving pictures came on the scene, Portsmouth was well in the fore in providing the latest entertainment for its patrons. The old Gladstone Buildings in Commercial Road — designed by Portsmouth architect A. E. Cogswell and built in 1885 — had a meeting room called the Victoria Hall. In July 1896 the first moving picture show was presented. This was only

PORTSDOWN FAIR, 1930. *The summer fair on the hill slopes above Cosham was always a popular day out in the late Twenties and early Thirties. Originally the fair was an extension of the old Free Mart Fair held at Point, Old Portsmouth. Fairground traders would often stop at the hill for a further two or three days after leaving Portsmouth and this casual gathering became accepted as an annual event. By the turn of the century the fair was the highlight of the year for many local people and was visited by itinerant traders from a wide area. As time progressed the trading side of the fair diminished and it became just an ordinary fun-fair with sideshows and the usual entertainments.*

THE PICTURE HOUSE,
COMMERCIAL ROAD,
PORTSMOUTH, 1915. *This
superb photograph shows the
ornate frontage of the Picture
House cinema, which stood in
Commercial Road between
Edinburgh Road and Stanhope
Road. It was opened on 16
December, 1913, and boasted a
marble lobby with oak panelling
and paintings of scenes from
naval history. The luxurious
interior was complemented by
the latest equipment including
special ventilation filters to
disperse smoke in case of fire,
and the most modern projectors
— guaranteed to be free from
vibration — were installed. A
few days after the opening, on
Saturday, 20 December, there
was a disastrous fire in the
Dockyard which destroyed the
Semaphore Tower and in which
two men died. On the following
Monday the cinema was
showing newsreel of the closing
stages of the blaze — quite a
scoop in those days. However the
cinema had a short life, for it
closed in the mid-Twenties and
lay derelict until 1936 when
sadly it was demolished for
redevelopment.*

a very basic production, but by August of the same year Portsmouth patrons were able to see an early newsreel — "The Prince of Wales's Horse Winning the Derby" on the large screen.

Later the hall was converted into a proper cinema and despite two serious fires in 1909 and 1911, continued to attract filmgoers until 1960. The last film starred Cliff Richard in "Expresso Bongo".

During the heyday of the picture palace, Portsmouth itself boasted as many as 40 cinemas, with more at Cosham, Waterlooville, Gosport, Havant, and Fareham.

Today leisure and pleasure is a major industry, generating more money than the huge manufacturing industries whose workers first gave free-time pleasure its golden boom years.

Above : LAKE ROAD, PORTSMOUTH, c.1900. The original Princes Theatre was opened in 1872. The original facade, before Frank Matcham's alterations of 1907 , can be seen behind the horse-drawn tram. Note the ornate gas street lamps at top left and the Edwardian gentleman who is wisely making a detour around the workmen's ladders.

Left : LAKE ROAD, PORTSMOUTH, 1940. This photograph shows the result of the air raid which led to the demise of the Princes Theatre. In 1907 a new owner, John Boughton, had commississioned a redesign and refurbishment of the theatre by Frank Matcham. The interior fittings were replaced with plush new ones and the theatre was equipped with electric lighting. A 93-foot cast iron balcony, similar to one at the Theatre Royal, was erected and the windows refitted with stained glass. There was a lounge for ladies and a tea room and a new saloon bar was constructed at the second-tier level. The Princes finally closed as a theatre in 1924, but was later reopened as a cinema. It was sold again in 1930 for £30,000 to a local cinema proprietor, Joe Davison, and lasted until the fateful afternoon of 24 August, 1940, when the Luftwaffe finally brought the house down.

SOUTH PARADE PIER, 1952. The band plays to a sparse audience, but in the best show-business tradition, the end-of-the pier show must go on. Many entertainers who went on to become household names started their careers in this type of show and many would have played at Southsea at one time or another. Although shows of this type were popular before the war, in the late Fifties, with the advent of television, they began to close. The South Parade Pier's own theatre was also a venue for many famous names, with concert parties in the summer and repertory and pantomime in the winter months. It originally seated 1450, but after alterations to the stage, this was reduced to 1,200.

Left : SOUTH PARADE PIER, 1890. This was the first South Parade Pier which was constructed in 1879 and was supposed to be fireproof. However in 1904 the unforeseen happened and the pier was all but destroyed. By 1908 a magnificent new construction was opened which saw good service to the people of Portsmouth and for holidaymakers. In 1974, during the shooting of the Ken Russell film 'Tommy', a fire broke out and damage estimated at £500,000 was done to the pier. However, like the phoenix rising from the ashes, the pier was rebuilt and is still a great attraction for seafront visitors today.

Above : CHILDREN'S CORNER, SOUTHSEA, 1929. *Interested parents watch their offspring enjoying themselves at the Children's Corner, near Southsea Castle. Pleasures were simple then — a sand pit, a set of swings and one or two slides — all very patriotic with the huge flags. And a ride on the model railway was a must. The narrow-gauge railway completes a circular tour around the entire play area and even in these days of electronic games and videos, the little railway still brings pleasure to the young ones.*

Right : HILSEA LIDO, 1947. *The Lido was officially opened on 24 July, 1935, by the then Lord Mayor Frank Privett. It boasted a promenade, paddling pool, water chutes and the only ten-metre diving tower in Hampshire. It had a cafe, sunbathing areas, floodlights for night swimming and a water polo area. There was dressing accommodation for more than 1,000 people. The complex took nine months to build and cost £40,000 — a great sum in those days. The late Thirties were days of sport and fitness and the Lido prospered. However the war put paid to its success and although it remained open it was never the same. It closed for repairs after the war and reopened in 1947, but never really made a repeat of the success it had previously enjoyed.*

Left : CANOE LAKE, SOUTHSEA, 1937. Sailing model boats on the Canoe Lake is still a popular pastime, although these enthusiasts are obviously in the big league. The Canoe Lake was constructed in the development of Southsea that took place in the 1880s, when the council obtained land from the War Office. The Ladies' Mile, the South Parade ornamental gardens and the lake were added to Portsmouth's list of amenities. In addition to the boats, the Canoe Lake once boasted a swannery.

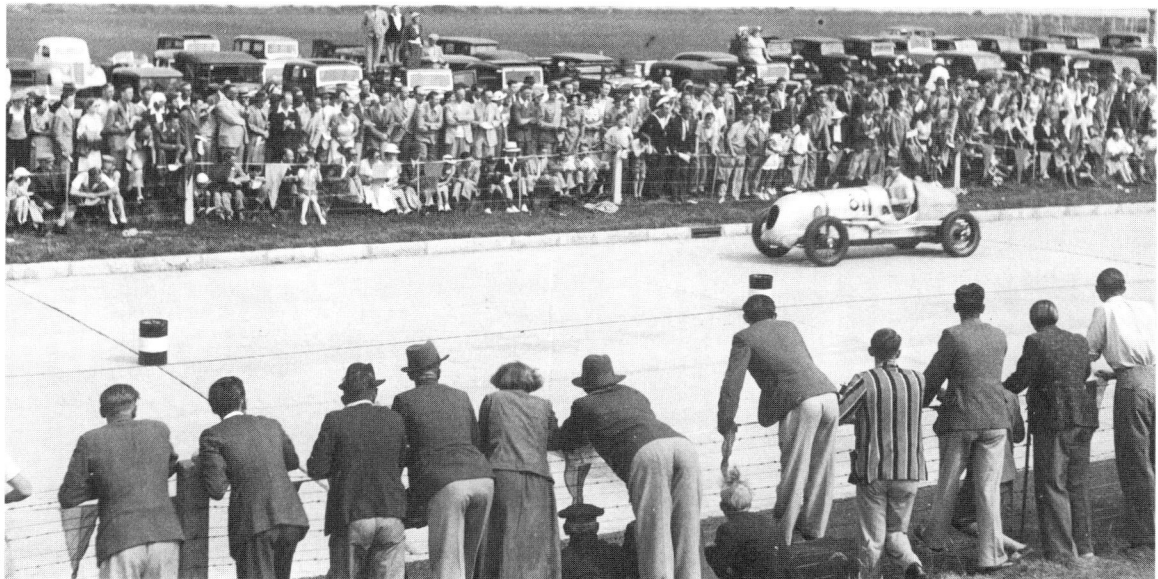

Left : EASTERN ROAD, PORTSMOUTH, 1932. After the First World War work commenced on the new Eastern Road, but was completed only as far as the golf course and what later became the airport. The work was curtailed because of the depression which hit the country in the Thirties. Work did not restart on the only other main road on to Portsea Island until November 1934, when the bridge over the creek was built, giving welcome employment to hundreds of Portsmouth workers. Between the wars motor racing and trials were popular spectator sports. Portsmouth catered for local enthusiasts by closing Eastern Road for the events.

Right : MODEL BOATING LAKE, GOSPORT, 1939. *Built on the site of the old Horsefields, the model boating lake was opened on August Bank Holiday, 1921. At four and a half acres it was reputed to be the largest artificial lake in the U.K. Three thousand people attended the opening ceremony, which ended with tub races and a procession of illuminated craft. The lake was used by the Gosport Model Yacht Club, which became famous for its competition successes, leading to the use of the lake at Gosport as a venue for many international events.*

Left : GOSPORT SWIMMING POOL 1930. *The open-air baths at Gosport were built on the site of the town ramparts and opened on 30 May, 1924. Costumes could be hired, but with 'B of G' emblazoned on the front they were not too popular. In 1936 a great deal of improvement took place, with new filtration and aeration machinery and additional changing facilities. Floodlights were installed for evening swimming and the baths were often the venue for regattas and water pageants. Sadly the swimming pool has disappeared with development of the area.*

PORTSMOUTH SWIMMING CLUB, 1913. Enjoying a dip in the briny are members of the ladies' branch of Portsmouth Swimming Club. Sea bathing became popular off Quebec House at the harbour entrance during the middle of the 19th Century. The sport's popularity remained consistent and subsequently a club was founded by Harry William Fisk in 1875. It was later to become the largest of its kind in the country and boasted nearly 1,500 members. Summer visitors were permitted to use the facilities for a nominal charge. The club's large wooden bathing stages — separate ones for men and women — were sited along the esplanade near Clarence Pier.

Left : SOUTHSEA COMMON, 1888. These doughty members of Southsea Tricycle Club are pictured on Southsea Common. Blazers, boaters and pocket watches and Albert chains were obviously the order of the day for the three-wheeler men, who boast only one clean-shaven member among them. Members of the Port of Portsmouth Bicycle Club, which was founded in 1879, entered into the spirit of things in a far more uniform way. They were clad in dark blue serge tunics, knickerbockers, dark grey stockings and polo caps upon which was displayed their elaborate emblem.

Above : PORTSMOUTH CYCLISTS, ISLE OF WIGHT, 1897. Portsmouth cycling enthusiasts are pictured here on a day out at Lisle Court. When the first cycling clubs were founded they were men-only affairs and many did not allow women to join until the late Twenties. However, here is a mixed bag of bicyclists, young and old and of both sexes. The ladies of the group, with their high-necked blouses and long skirts, evoke comparison with Miss Violet Smith in one of Sherlock Holmes's most baffling investigations — The Case of the Solitary Cyclist.

PORTSMOUTH ROAD, COSHAM, 1904. This picture, taken on 13 July, 1904, shows 60 men and boys at the ready for the shop assistants' walk. The temperature was in the seventies, even at 4.55 pm when the event started. From Cosham the walkers proceeded to the foot of Portsdown Hill and through East Cosham, Drayton and on to Bedhampton where the competitors turned at the Belmont Tavern. They then went up the hill and along to the George and then down through North End to the Town Hall. The total distance was 10·5 miles, and the winner completed the course in 1 hour 28 minutes.

Above and right : WYLLIE'S STUDIO, BROAD STREET, OLD PORTSMOUTH, c. 1929. W. L. Wyllie, R.A., lived at No.1 Tower House in Old Portsmouth with an adjoining studio both of which were built on the site of a stable building once used by the tramways. This studied pose shows him with his wife, son and daughter, who were also artists. The address of his studio was unique — the only address in the world which could not be copied — for over the archway, retained from the stables, was the inscription of the exact latitude and longitude. The Post Office delivered many letters addressed to 'Mr. Wyllie, Lat. 50° 47' 25" North — Long. 1° 6' 25" West'. Although the building was badly damaged in the last war the arch can still be seen today. Wyllie painted seascapes and naval battles and his panorama of Trafalgar was presented to the nation shortly before his death. Mr. Wyllie was held in such esteem by the local community and by the Navy that the latter accorded him full naval honours at his funeral on 6 April, 1931.

Following page : THE MUDLARKS, PORTSEA, 1935. Right up to the early Sixties, before the redevelopment of the viaduct from The Hard to the Harbour Station and the Gosport and Isle of Wight ferry pontoons, visitors and travellers could while away a few spare moments by stopping to watch the antics of the mudlarks. Young boys and in this case even young men would dive into the black, squelchy mud to retrieve coppers thrown from the walkway above. Occasionally one would come up with something different, such as the horn of a gramophone as seen in this picture. A 1950 film, 'The Mudlark,' starring Andrew Ray and Anthony Steel, brought their activities to a much wider audience.

GETTING ABOUT

THE WORLD today is a very small place — modern air transport has shrunk even the longest journey to mere hours. Foreign holidays are commonplace, most families have a car and the public transport network makes travelling easy. So it is hard to imagine a time when getting about was so difficult that only the really wealthy could even contemplate it.

The first great change came about with the development of the canal, which enabled both goods and people to be transported cheaply. From about 1760 until the end of the canal hey-day about 4,000 miles of navigable waterways were constructed. Although the vast majority of canals were situated in the industrial midlands and the north, the Portsmouth area did not miss out.

In fact at Titchfield can be seen the remains of what is thought to be the second oldest canal in the country. Titchfield was a thriving port, but when in 1611 the Earl of Southampton blocked the mouth of the Meon and built a canal from the village to the coast, it caused a public outcry. The earl's purpose was to convey goods to and from his mill and tannery and to irrigate the nearby farmland. However, the blocking of the estuary put paid to Titchfield's port possibilities.

Another watery venture in the south, which also came to nought, was the development of the Portsmouth and Arundel Canal. The work on the waterway began in 1818 and it was originally planned to link Portsmouth with London via the Wey and Arun Canal, the River Wey and the Thames.

The canal entered Portsea Island at Milton, where the remains of the lock gates can still be seen and ran to the canal basin just off the present-day Commercial Road. Arundel Street was named in honour of the canal's eventual destination.

The grand opening took place on 26 May, 1823, with great celebrations and pomp. Sadly it was not a success and when residents complained that it was polluting their drinking water, it was drained and eventually filled in when the railways came. The railway cutting at Fratton still follows the line of the canal and Fratton Bridge was built on the site of one of the original canal crossings, Kerth Bridge. It was the railways of course that killed the waterways as viable commercial operations.

Rail travel hit the peak of its importance in 1842, when Queen Victoria first travelled to Windsor by train. For the poor, rail travel was an uncomfortable business. Third-class carriages were open to the smoke and soot, and the seats were just hard, wooden benches — very different to the first-class rolling stock, which boasted upholstered seats, curtains and mirrors.

The physical effects of actually building the railways had a profound effect on the countryside. Viaducts, tunnels, bridges, stations and huge cuttings through acres of land, altered the appearance of countryside which had been virtually unchanged for centuries.

POINT, OLD PORTSMOUTH, 1931. *A Gosport ferry boat, obviously on a 'Round-the-harbour' special, awaits passengers at Point, Old Portsmouth. The shoreline shows a number of the many hostelries found on Spice Island, as Old Portsmouth was often called. On the left is the Star and Garter hotel, famous for its window upon which so many naval heroes — Nelson included — had scratched their names. The Union Tavern with the 'Brickwoods' sign on the side stands next to the Coal Exchange, while across Bath Square is the Still and West Country House. Out on the far point to the right is the wooden structure of the Coastguard's hailing station.*

And there were further effects on the population. People were now able to see other parts of the country in which they lived, and many who had never travelled more than a few miles from home were able to see first-hand how their fellow countrymen lived.

The large towns and cities began to spread, forming suburbs, encouraged by the ease of travel into the cities. For the first time workers began to live away from their places of work and the cheap fares gained for the railway companies a whole new generation of customers — commuters.

The rail companies were gradually taking the freight business formerly enjoyed by the canals. The waterway systems began to amalgamate in their fight for survival. The Grand Junction Canal, the Regent Canal and several other minor routes amalgamated to become the Grand Union. However their efforts were largely futile, and one-by-one they closed.

Today the canals are enjoying a new hey-day. Many of the better preserved systems have been fully restored to be exploited for their leisure potential. Others are being considered as conduits for the movement of scarce water resources from one part of the country to another.

The first railway in the Portsmouth area was the London to Southampton link to Gosport, which opened in 1841. This was a tiresome experience for Portsmouth travellers who were forced to take the floating bridge to Gosport, and then a carriage for the further half-mile to the town's grandiose station.

This put Portsmouth at a disadvantage with Southampton, and severely hampered its prospects as a commercial port. However these prospects improved when the London, Brighton, and South Coast Railway opened a line from Brighton to Portsmouth in 1847.

Meanwhile the London and South Western Railway made plans to extend its line from Fareham, through Portchester, and to continue down the western shore of Portsea Island through the little villages of Rudmore and Mile End. In the event the two companies' lines merged at Cosham at a place still known today as the Railway Triangle.

By the end of the 19th Century the railway companies were all-powerful, but even they were not to know that their motive system would soon be overtaken by another — the internal combustion engine.

Previous page : PORTSMOUTH HARBOUR, 1935. Passengers disembarking from the Gosport ferry at the Hard. It is interesting to note the huge pile of bicycles stacked at the bow. In the background is the railway viaduct leading across to the South Railway Jetty, sometimes known as the Farewell Jetty. The line linked the Dockyard with the Harbour Station and was often used when Royal passengers were leaving from Portsmouth. The ferry boat just arriving is the Varos, one of a series of vessels with names beginning with the letter V. The other were Vesta, Vadne and Vita.

Right : GOSPORT FERRY, 1900. Frances, one of the ferryboats of the Gosport and Portsea Watermen's Steam Launch Company, prepares to leave for Portsmouth. The company was formed in 1875 by a group of independent watermen who were faced with loss of trade from steam launches operated by the floating bridge company. The watermen started with six boats — Lily, Grand Duchess, Marquis of Lorne, Princess Louise, Elfin and Frances — each acquired from individual boatmen in return for shares in the company.

Meanwhile the need for a more localised transport system within Portsmouth and the surrounding villages was paramount.

The early record of public transport in Portsmouth goes back to about 1840 when a horse-bus service ran between North End and Southsea. In the succeeding years various horse-drawn services operated routes in and around Portsmouth — in fact some were still running as late as 1920. The omnibuses were succeeded by horse-drawn trams and the 1865 line between Town Station and Clarence Pier is regarded as the first statutory tramway in the country. In 1900, Portsmouth Corporation took over the line under the Street Tramways Act, and the stage was set for real progress and for the following 30 years Portsmouth Corporation Tramways was a highly successful business.

The system was later electrified which caused disruption to the business of the town as lines were laid and cable poles were erected. The first electric tram was due to run on 19 September, 1901, but because of other events the ceremony was put off until September 24.

Drivers' pay was set at £1.5s. (£1·25) for a 63-hour week and the conductor earned £1.2s. (£1·10) per week.

Left : PORTSMOUTH HARBOUR, 1900. A horse-drawn cart disembarks from the floating bridge Duchess of York at Gosport. The harbour link was very important for traders on both sides of the harbour — a tuppenny fare saved much wear and tear on both vehicles and animals. The Duchess was the last vessel to be built for the company and did sterling work until 1959, when she and her sister ship were in such a bad state of repair that the company suspended the service. Sadly the days of the chain ferries were ended and the company never resumed operations and was wound up in 1960.

The *Evening News* reported the inauguration, saying: "A new era in the sytem of locomotion in the main thoroughfares of Portsmouth is to be inaugurated today, by the opening of the electric tramway for the public service. The event has long been anticipated and we feel sure that the enterprise and spirit which prompted the corporation to embark upon such a huge undertaking will be fully justified by the results."

But the era of the tram was not to last. The first motor buses ran in tandem with the trams from 1919, and over the following years the trams were gradually phased out, the last one running on November 10, 1936, with due pomp and circumstance. Four trams ran in convoy, driven for part of the way by the Lord Mayor, Frederick Spickernell.

Meanwhile the corporation had decided to introduce trolley buses to Portsmouth and the first one ran on 4 August, 1934. Trolleys, which took their power from overhead cables, were quiet and comparatively cheap to run. One of their faults however, was dewiring, when the pick-up arms became detached from the cables. For that purpose a long bamboo pole was carried beneath each vehicle to enable the conductor to replace the arm.

The trolleys carried on through the war years and were eventually phased out, the last trolley running on 27 July, 1963, leaving the road clear for the motor bus more or less as we know it today.

It is obvious that methods of transport have changed considerably since the beginning of Victoria's reign, but the development of air travel has been the most momentous.

People really bacame aware of the possibilities of air travel during the First World War with the exploits of the Royal Flying Corps. After the war those who could afford it became eager to

try this new form of transport and by 1919 joy rides were being offered.

On the commercial side a number of airlines were formed, many of which merged in 1927 into Imperial Airways, which via British European Airways and combined with British Overseas Airways Corporation eventually emerged as British Airways.

Portsmouth entered the new air age in 1932 when land at Highgrove, on the eastern boundary, was earmarked for a new airport. It opened on 2 July, 1932, with a huge air display and a controversial visit from the Graf Zeppelin. Flights were run to the Isle of Wight on a regular basis, and within a few years the airport was in the news again when it was chosen as the turning point for the King's Cup air race.

On 11 July of the same year it welcomed its first Royal visitors when the Prince of Wales and Prince George arrived in two Puss Moth aeroplanes.

The airport suspended operations during the war, but soon came back back to life with increased peace time activity. In 1955, Channel Airways started a regular service to the Channel

Islands — an operation which lasted until 1967, when two events on the same day decided the fate of the airport. On 15 August two Hawker Siddeley 748 turboprops — one from Southend and the other from Jersey — came to grief in torrential rain on the grass runway. Although there were no casualties, the accidents prompted safety investigations and the constraints put upon craft landing at Portsmouth prompted Channel Airways to move its operations to Southend.

The yo-yo airport — as it was dubbed — remained devoid of services until 1971 when another attempt to to run flights to Jersey was started. However, by the next year it became apparent that the airport was not profitable and it finally closed on 31 December, 1973, bringing to an end the whole spectrum of air transport development in Portsmouth.

Now the latest craze in 'people moving' is for light rapid transit systems. Plans are afoot to construct a system from Portsmouth around the harbour to Gosport, in a bid to alleviate the road congestion experienced by commuters. So perhaps public transport will turn full circle and a modern equivalent of the tram will be seen on the streets of Portsmouth.❦

Left : PORTSMOUTH HARBOUR, 1935. This aerial view of the harbour shows one of the chain ferries or floating bridges making its way from Gosport to Portsmouth. These huge craft were a neccessary alternative to the long journey around the harbour when they started operations in May 1840, with one vessel, the Victoria. The venture was such a success that by 1842 the Albert joined the fleet. Each was 100 feet long with a beam of 60 feet and they were propelled by two steam engines which ran on chains over oak cogs for quieter operation. In 1864 the Victoria was replaced by the Alexandra and in 1892 the Duchess of York was brought into operation. The one in the picture is probably the Alexandra.

Above : BROAD STREET, OLD PORTSMOUTH, c.1905. This picture shows a similar view to the photograph on the following page but it was taken just after the turn of the century. Vehicles here are waiting to board the floating bridge to Gosport. The building on the right of the picture is the Star and Garter Hotel, famous for its connections with such eminent seafarers as Nelson, Howe and Sir John Franklin. The hotel stood until January 1954, when it was demolished.

Left : GOSPORT FERRY PONTOON, 1937. A ferry boat arrives as another leaves for Portsmouth. As the final bell would ring, it was a familiar sight to see the latecomers racing down the pontoon to try to reach the boat before the chain was drawn across. The entire foredeck was usually crammed with dockyardmen's cycles and while the journey was pleasant on a fine day, in wet weather it was quite an experience to be packed into the hot lower cabin. In the left background, moored at the South Railway Jetty, is the Royal yacht, Victoria and Albert.

Left : BROAD STREET. OLD PORTSMOUTH, 1927. Intrepid motorists wait at the Broad Street slipway for vehicles to disembark from the new Isle of Wight ferry, Fishbourne. The Fishbourne was the first drive-on drive-off vessel on the Island route. The small knot of spectators obviously found the sight interesting, or perhaps they were foot passengers themselves. Ryde had been proving difficult for goods traffic because at low water the tide went out almost as far as the pier, so in 1925 Southern Railway purchased two acres of land at Wootton Creek and made preparations for the new service. The Fishbourne cost £13,254 and was launched on 2 June, 1927, and came into service during August of the same year. She could carry 15 cars at any one time and there were separate ladies' and gentlemen's saloons.

Right : GOSPORT STATION, 1941. The hugely ornate Gosport station is pictured during the war years, the atmosphere reinforced by the barrage balloon high in the sky. The governor of the town in the 19th Century would not allow the railway to enter the then fortified area and as a result the station was situated half a mile from the ferry terminal. The station was designed by Sir William Tite and comprised a stone and granite colonnade in Italian Tuscan style. In the early days of rail travel, passengers had to enter their names and destinations in a book. This was done in the Book-in Office, from where the term Booking Office was supposedly derived.

DENMEAD, 1890. A family outing in a four-wheeler at Denmead with the lady of the household taking the reins. Whether the woman on the tricycle is part of the group seems doubtful. Behind them is Denmead windmill. The mill was said to have been built in 1819 and worked as a windmill proper until about 1900 when the sails were removed. It stood in an emasculated condition until 1922 when it was demolished. For many years there was a colourful smear on the brickwork, caused when a paint pot was spilled while the woodwork was being painted. From this point the towers of three other windmills could be seen. Two at Hambledon and one which still stands, 650 ft. above sea level, on Chalton Hill. This last mill was built at the start of the last century but it is said that a series of mills have stood there since 1289. Chalton Mill was derelict until 1978 when it was skillfully converted into living accomodation with a new cap and sails.

Below :
PORTSMOUTH,
c.1925. A
Portsmouth taxi of
the London cab
type, complete
with wire spoke
wheels and a fold-
down soft top for
warmer days. The
driver also had a
top to protect
himself from the
weather but this is
of the roll-down
type, which was
attached to the
windscreen.

Above : FRATTON STATION, 1925. A 'new-fangled' taxi and a
couple of horse-drawn cabs await passengers alighting at Fratton.
The enclosed four-wheeled cab, drawn by one horse, was known as
a Clarence cab. During the 1820s coach manufacturer David
Davies of Albany built small, closed, town carriages which became
popular as family coaches and hackney vehicles. They were known
as Clarences after the Duke of Clarence — later William IV —
who ordered one of the first examples. Because of their capacity the
Clarences were ideal for the railway station trade, where a larger
vehicle than a Hansom was needed. These cabs were often known
as growlers, because of the sound the iron-rimmed wheels made on
the road surface. The use of Clarences persisted, with many still
being seen in London up to 1939.

COSHAM, 1910. A Portsdown and Horndean Light Railway tram negotiates the double track section west of Cosham. Fort Widley dominates the summit of Portsdown Hill in the background. The building on the left of the picture is the Queen Alexandra Hospital for Wounded Soldiers. Building began in 1904 and the hospital received its first patients in 1908. Special ambulances were brought from Aldershot and patients were brought in from as far as Weymouth, Dorchester and Winchester. In 1926 the Ministry of Pensions took over the hospital for the care of disabled service personnel from the Great War. It continued in this role until 1941 when the first civilian patients were admitted as a result of bomb damage to the Royal Hospital. In the following year two land mines put the Royal completely out of action and even more patients were transferred to the 'QA'. By 1950 the hospital was treating a majority of civilian patients.

Left : PORTSDOWN HILL, 1930. A Portsdown and Horndean Light Railway tram at the summit of Portsdown Hill, by the George Inn. The R. A. C. man on point duty has just waved the vehicle on, as it makes its journey down the south side of the hill and on to Portsmouth. Through-running to Portsmouth started in August 1924, with trams to the Town Hall. This service was eventually extended to South Parade Pier. The last car to run on the light railway did so on 9 January, 1935, and the tracks were eventually pulled up. The iron bridge over the Southwick Hill road is the only reminder of a popular undertaking. Note the advertising for Streten & Janner's milk adorning each of the steps to the upper deck.

Right : WEST STREET, FAREHAM, 1920. The tramway came late to Fareham. The electric service was installed in Gosport after a lengthy wrangle between the council and Mr. A. W. White, the owner of the original horse-drawn service. The council wished to compulsarily purchase the trams, so a dispute developed which White eventually won. He sought permission to extend the Gosport line to Fareham, Portchester and Cosham, but in the event the tramway terminated at Fareham, mainly because of strong opposition from the London and South Western Railway Company. A new power station was built at Hoeford and the first tram ran on 27 October, 1905.

WATERLOOVILLE, 1919. Wadham Brothers won an important post-war contract for ten double-decker open-top buses for Portsmouth Corporation Tramways. Here five of the first six Thornycroft J-type 36-seaters are standing outside the Heroes of Waterlooville on 1 August, 1919. After about six years the bodies developed problems, no doubt because of the condition of the roads combined with the solid tyres and hard suspension. The Wadhams bodies were replaced with second-hand bodies from the London General Omnibus Company at a cost of £25 each. The first motor bus route started on 11 August, 1919, and ran between Devonshire Avenue, the Dockyard, Arundel Street and St Mary's Road. Vehicle No. 10, now renumbered No. 1, is owned by Portsmouth Museums.

DOCKYARD GATE, 1905. Trams are pictured outside the Dockyard Main Gate, awaiting seamen from the French Fleet. The trams were decorated in honour of an auspicious occasion. This visit in August 1905, often referred to as the 'Entente Cordiale Review', came within a few weeks of the 100th anniversary of the Battle of Trafalgar. The French fleet, under Admiral Caillard, comprising 12 vessels, moored abreast of ships of the English Channel Fleet. The fleets were reviewed by the Lords of the Admiralty, aboard the Admiralty yacht Enchantress and by King Edward, Queen Alexandra and the Prince and Princess of Wales, aboard the Royal Yacht Victoria and Albert.

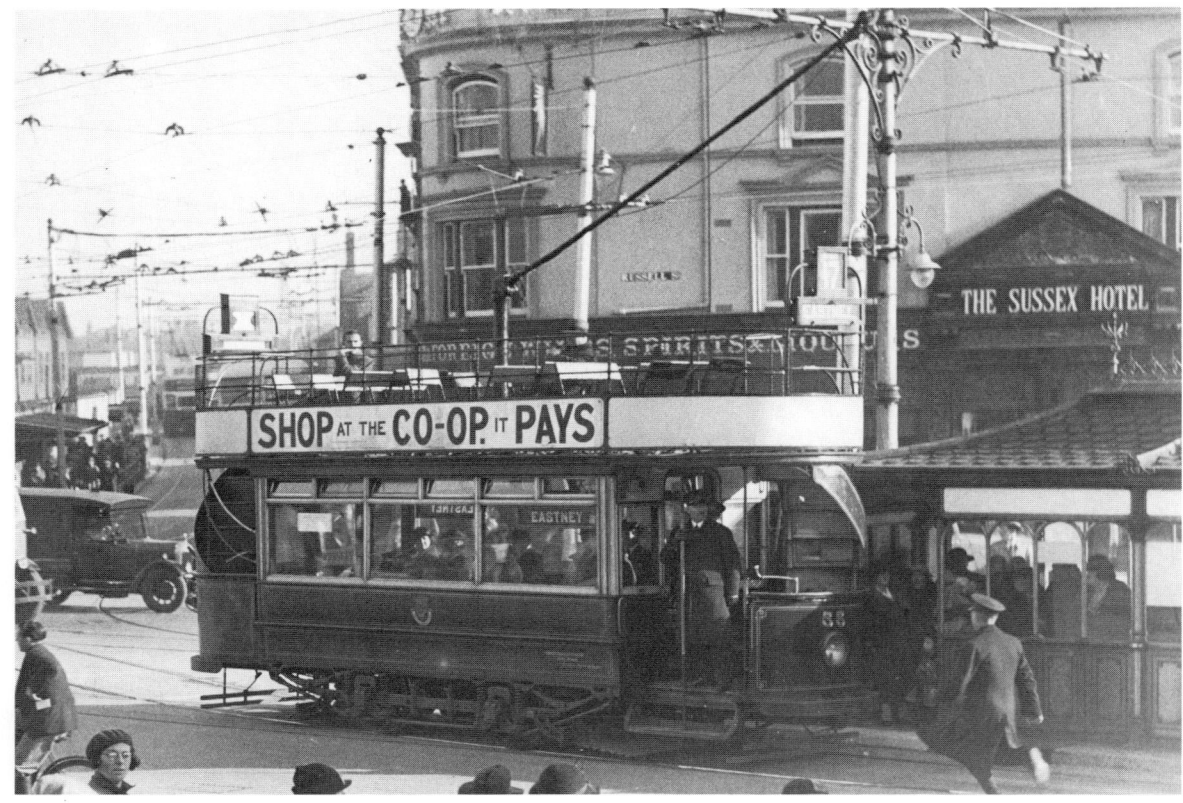

These three photographs show the tram when it was a common form of transport — much respected and relied on by the people of Portsmouth and the surrounding areas. All the vehicles carry route numbers, which replaced the earlier letter system on 18 July, 1927.

Above : SUSSEX HOTEL, RUSSELL STREET, c.1935. This photograph must have been taken rather late in the day for the tram, as a trolley bus can be seen in the background in Greetham Street. It shows a tram on route 17, outside the Sussex Hotel in the Guildhall Square. Both Greetham Street and the hotel disappeared in the redevelopment of the Guildhall area and the subsequent construction of the Civic Offices. The handsome, pagoda-like tram shelter, to the right of the picture, was built like many in the city, by the Westminster firm of David Rowell.

Below : SOUTHSEA. This photograph shows a pair of trams on the Dockyard — South Parade Pier — Eastney route. They are pictured passing by the Ladies' Mile at Southsea.

Above : COMMERCIAL ROAD, PORSTMOUTH. A No. 2 tram is pictured in a busy Commercial Road, near the junction with Charlotte Street. The No. 2 carried pasengers on the Cosham, Guildhall and Clarence Pier route.

Left : THE LAST TRAM, PORTSMOUTH, 1936. The last tram ran from the Guildhall, Portsmouth, on 10 November, 1936. There were four cars in the procession and the final one carried the words 'Journey's End' on its destination board. Local people stood still and silent and with heads bared, as the vehicles travelled past at a funereal pace. At the Greetham Street meat market, butchers showed their respect by clanging their cleavers, which were suspended on ropes from the beams. In his speech the chairman of the Passenger Transport Committee, John Timpson, said: 'Portsmouth is parting today with a very good and valuable friend'. (The badge numbers of these men are as follows : 456, 445, 504, 62, 14, 227, 454, 513 and 447.)

Top left, page 131: LAST GOSPORT TRAM, 1929. The first tram ran in Gosport on 17 July, 1882, and they continued to serve the community until 1929. This picture shows Car No. 8 making its last journey to Ann's Hill from Fareham on December 31, 1929. Car No. 1 carried a wreath throughout the final day. At the time of closure there were 20 of the original 22 cars surviving — seven were transferred to the Portsdown and Horndean Light Railway, while another six went to the Great Grimsby Street Tramways Company.

Below : FRATTON ROAD, 1938. Passengers outside St. Mary's Church board a trolley bus for South Parade Pier. The trolleys had only been in operation for four years and were still something of a

novelty. Kingston Road and Fratton Road were popular shopping areas — the Co-operative House department store was a firm favourite which attracted customers from far and wide. Many of these were Co-operative Society members who twice-yearly queued to collect their dividend. The store stood until fairly recently, but has now been replaced by a modern undercover shopping complex.

Above : NORTH END, 1934. An experimental trolley bus — a twin rear-axled Sunbeam — is pictured at North End junction. The trolleys, using current from overhead wires, were introduced on August 4, 1934. The wiring system at Fratton Bridge was said to be the most complicated in the country. The buses were cheap to run and extremely quiet in operation. The latter fact sadly proven on 12 December, 1934, when a Royal Marines pensioner stepped out in front of a trolley and was killed instantly. At the coroner's court a verdict of accidental death was brought in and the driver was exonerated of all blame.

Left : PORTCHESTER STATION, 1930. The castellated roofline of the station building is rather reminiscent of the more famous landmark on the foreshore. This clear view of the village's upside-down station is now obscured, as houses now stand where the fence is. The platform and booking office is on the high level, while other offices and living accommodation are on the lower level. The line through Portchester was part of the old London and South Western Railway. The company planned a line to Portsmouth via Portchester and Cosham, but eventually abandoned its plans at Cosham, at the point known as the Railway Triangle. The line was to have been extended to the little villages of Mile End and Rudmore.

Left : PORTSMOUTH AND SOUTHSEA STATION, 1938. Steam reigns in this evocative picture taken at the beginning of the war. At this time it was a case of : 'Is your journey really necessary?' The Guildhall, with its minarettes can be seen through the steam to the far left of the picture. The cluster of little houses on the right show what the area looked like before the Second World War bombs did their damage. The Portsmouth line terminated here until 1876 when the high-level extension to Portsmouth Harbour was constructed. A move probably bought about by the popularity of the Isle of Wight as a holiday resort — influenced no doubt by Queen Victoria's love for the island. The Dockyard also took advantage of the waterside extension with the opening of the line to the South Railway Jetty — a familiar route for royal trains. The letters PER — Portsmouth Extension Railway — are wrought into the iron roof brackets of the high-level platform.

Left : PORTSMOUTH AND SOUTHSEA STATION, 1952. A steam train pulls in to the high-level platform, watched by two young travellers.

Below : GOSPORT ROAD STATION, 1925. Trains for Stokes Bay originally went to Gosport Station and then shunted out backwards. To avoid this a new curved section was constructed, coming into operation on 1 June, 1865. On the same day a new station, Stoke Road, was opened. It later became known as Gosport Road. In 1889 the platforms were lengthened. This unusual view shows the 'Up' platform looking south.

Left : EAST SOUTHSEA STEAM RAILCAR, 1910. By the middle of the last century Southsea was beginning to become popular as a watering place, so it was considered a rail link to the main line would be an asset. It took until 1884 to actually start the work but the track was completed within a year. It ran from Fratton station to the East Southsea terminus at what is now Granada Road and was officially opened on 1 July, 1885. Each locomotive was yellow with a black smokestack with a copper band. However the Portsmouth trams proved to be stiff competition and within a very few years the rail company cut its losses and made the line single track and introduced steam railcars. These were never a real success and by 1914 the last passengers were carried and the line was closed.

Left : MEON VALLEY RAILWAY, 1955. An Alton train is seen leaving Droxford station in February of that year. During the building of the station in 1900, one of the navvies unearthed a skeleton. The police were called and all work was suspended while the authorities considered the possibility of a murder investigation. However, a Southampton antiquary, William Dale, was consulted and he confirmed after discussions with the British Museum, that the bones were of Anglo-Saxon origin. Mr. Dale visited the site on a number of occasions and with the help, as he condescendingly put it, of 'a couple of navvies who were more intelligent than was usual with their class, excavated a quantity of artefacts, including spear heads, a gilt bronze brooch and an iron and silver belt buckle. Droxford station had its shining hour during the war, in June 1944. The long platform was suitable to host the special train which housed the war cabinet while the final preparations for D-Day were being made. The train, with Churchill, Eisenhower, De Gaulle and Eden amongst those on board, stayed at the heavily guarded station for two days.

A Portsmouth Bibliography

A CITY AT WAR, Nigel Peake, Milestone (Horndean) 1988.

CROSSING THE HARBOUR The Portsmouth Harbour Story, Lesley Burton and Brian Musselwhite, Milestone (Horndean) 1986.

FARES PLEASE The History of Passenger Transport in Portsmouth, Eric Watts, Milestone (Horndean) 1987.

HAMPSHIRE MURDERS, Roger Guttridge, Ensign (Southampton) 1990.

An ILLUSTRATED HISTORY OF FAREHAM, Lesley Burton and Brian Musselwhite, Ensign (Southampton) 1991.

KEEP THE HOME FIRES BURNING, John Sadden, Portsmouth Printing & Publishing Ltd. (Portsmouth) 1990.

LITERARY WALKS in the South Country, John Price, Portsmouth Printing & Publishing Ltd. (Portsmouth) 1988.

The MEON VALLEY RAILWAY, R. A. Stone, Kingfisher (Southampton) 1983.

The NAVAL HERITAGE OF PORTSMOUTH, John Winton, Ensign (Southampton) 1989

NOTES ON THE TOPOGRAPHY OF PORTSMOUTH, Alexander Howell, Barrells (London) 1913.

The PLACE-NAMES OF HAMPSHIRE, Richard Coates, Batsford (London) 1989.

A PORTRAIT OF PORTSEA 1840-1940, Joy Harwood, Ensign (Southampton) 1990.

PORTSMOUTH : HISTORY IN HIDING, Anthony Triggs, Ensign (Southampton) 1989.

PORTSMOUTH NOT SO OLD, Richard Esmond, Gale and Polden (Portsmouth) 1961.

PORTSMOUTH PAST AND PRESENT, Anthony Triggs, Ensign (Southampton) 1988.

The PORTSMOUTH THAT HAS PASSED, William Gates, Ed. Nigel Peake, Milestone (Horndean) 1987.

PORTSMOUTH THEN AND NOW, Anthony Triggs, Milestone (Horndean) 1986.

One Hundred Years of ROADS AND RAILS AROUND THE SOLENT, David Fereday Glenn, Ensign (Southampton) 1991.

The STORY OF GOSPORT, Leonard White, Ed. Lesley Burton and Brian Musselwhite, Ensign (Southampton) 1989.

WATERLOOVILLE — A MODERN VILLAGE, Alison Marshall, Window Press (Waterlooville) 1983.

Photographic acknowledgements

All photographs in this book are from the author's collection except those listed below. These organisations and individuals are gratefully acknowledged :

British Museum of Road Transport : 105
Kay Edney : 83
Fareham Library : 125
Francis Frith Collection PLC* : 26, 38, 70, 90, 92, 113
Hampshire County Library : 4, 5, 40, 56, 82, 83
Imperial War Museum : 104
The News : 10, 17, 21, 29, 32, 35, 36, 59, 69(r), 76, 96, 100(r)
Portsmouth City Library : 30, 103, 106
Portsmouth City Records Office : 26, 63
Royal Commission on Historical Monuments (England) : 95
Keith Smith : 121, 134

*The story of **The Francis Frith Collection**, related elsewhere in this book, and the collection of photographs they manage, is now more strongly linked to Hampshire as the collection is now situated here. Copies of the photographs listed above and many, many more featuring other parts of Hampshire and of course the rest of Britain are available by post from **The Francis Frith Collection PLC, Charlton Road, Andover, Hampshire SP10 3LE. Telephone (Andover) 0264-353113**

Index of Place - Names